WORLD FOLKTALES

A Multicultural Approach to Whole Language

GRADES 6–8

By Jerry Mallett
and
Keith Polette

Alleyside Press
Fort Atkinson, Wisconsin

Published by Alleyside Press, an imprint of Highsmith Press
Highsmith Press
W5527 Highway 106
P.O. Box 800
Fort Atkinson, Wisconsin 53538-0800

1-800-558-2110

© Jerry Mallett and Keith Polette, 1994
Cover design: Frank Neu

The paper used in this publication meets the minimum requirements of
American National Standard for Information Science —
Permanence of Paper for Printed Library Material. ANSI/NISO Z39.48-1992.

Library of Congress Cataloging in Publication
  Mallet, Jerry J., 1939-
    World folktales : a multicultural approach to whole language /
  by Jerry Mallett and Keith Polette.
        p.   cm.
  Includes bibliographical references.
  Contents: [1] K-2 -- [2] 3-5 -- [3] 6-8.
  ISBN 0-917846-43-5 (v. 1 : alk. paper). --ISBN 0-917846-44-3
  (v. 2 : alk. paper). -- ISBN 0-917846-45-1 (v. 3 : alk. paper)
  1. Tales--Study and teaching (Elementary)--United States.
  2. Language experience approach in education--United States.
  3. Multicultural education--United States.
  I. Polette, Keith, 1954-   . II. Title.
  LB1576.M3625 1994
  372.64--dc20   94-21691

CONTENTS

INTRODUCTION

This book is based upon the premise that children learn most effectively and efficiently by becoming active participants in the process of education. Quite simply, this means that children learn least when they sit passively for hours and read and respond to material in which they are not both mentally and emotionally engaged. One approach which allows and encourages children to become more involved in learning is Whole Language. Whole Language is not a system, or a specific set of strategies, but is rather a different kind of educational orientation which places the student at the center of the learning situation. Consequently, Whole Language relies heavily upon the perceptions and experiences that the student brings to the classroom every day because these experiences are the base upon which Whole Language is built.

The activities in *World Folktales: A Multicultural Approach to Whole Language*, are designed to help the teacher create a Whole Language environment by using the experiences of the student as a bridge to increased literacy through active involvement. In addition, the activities are holistic in format, being based as they are upon a multiplicity of both productive and critical (higher order) thinking skills, which means that the whole student, not just an isolated part of his/her brain, will be engaged in learning.

The specific educational objectives of this book are for the student to: gain an appreciation for folktales as a literary genre; gain an increased understanding and appreciation of world cultures as expressed through their various folktales; demonstrate high order thinking processes with increased facility; acquire a higher level of literacy; develop more efficient writing, speaking and listening skills; develop the ability to respond to a literary text in a myriad of clear and purposeful ways; develop more sophisticated language patterns; and develop a strong working vocabulary.

The activities in this book are ready to be used in the language arts classroom without requiring a great deal of preparation time. Many are also designed to be enjoyable, to take the malaise that many students feel out of learning. Consequently, this book will help the teacher create a strong sense of "psychological safety" in the classroom. When students feel "safe," that is, when they feel that their experiences, perceptions and ideas are valid and acceptable, they will often see more purpose for reading, writing, speaking, listening and thinking in the classroom. The Whole Language approach allows the teacher to become more of a facilitator and to also make his/her job easier and more rewarding. When both the students and the teacher are relaxed, true learning begins.

BOOK ORGANIZATION

For easy use and clarity, *World Folktales: A Multicultural Approach to Whole Language* is arranged into the following eight cultural units:

Asian (China)

West European (Ireland)

Middle East/India (Afghanistan)

American Indian/Inuit

African American/Africa

East European (Romania)

Hispanic (Costa Rica)

Jewish/Yiddish

These eight cultural sections are organized into uniform units. Each unit begins with a folktale indigenous to that particular cultural group. This is followed by three activity sections emphasizing the whole-language approach: Before Reading Activities, During Reading Activities and After Reading Activities. Each unit is completed with student activity sheets which may be copied for immediate student use.

A "Story Integration" section may be found at the end of the book. This section is composed of Whole-Language activities which overlap and combine all of the folktales found here.

THE HUNGER FOR MUSIC

FOLKTALE FROM CHINA

Every autumn Emperor Po hosted a tremendous feast for members of his court and many of the wealthy merchants who lived near his palace and each year he would serve the most wonderful and exotic food that anyone had ever tasted. Because the feast had become such a tradition, many of the guests had grown so accustomed to the Emperor's generous treatment that they had become bored with the whole affair.

As the Emperor watched his guests arrive, he noticed that they were all arrayed in silk garments that shimmered like the wings of butterflies and wore jewels larger than birds' eggs. The guests were so busy chatting with one another that they did not notice the frown on Emperor Po's face.

After everyone was seated, the food was served. A parade of servants loaded the table with delicacies: roast duck glazed in honey, sizzling bird nest soup, stir-fried chicken smothered with plum sauce, and steamed vegetables sauteed with a secret spice the Emperor called *drops of the sun*. The guests took no notice of the food, but continued to chatter. Some yawned, while others dozed. One guest cleaned his fingernails while another tried to balance a chopstick on his forehead. Even the rich and pungent aromas failed to tickle the jaded guests' noses.

A gong sounded. The guests looked to the Emperor. He sat strangely still. He did nothing but eye his guests.

Finally, Li Ching, his minister of defense spoke up, "Excuse me, Your Highness, but shouldn't we eat now? The food grows cold."

The Emperor spoke, "All in good time. First I must ask you a question."

A feeling of hummingbirds fluttered in each of the guests' stomachs. This was something the Emperor had never done before.

The Emperor continued, "Who can tell me what the sweetest music is?"

For a long moment, no one spoke. Each guest looked around the room nervously, their eyes blinking, their mouths shut so tightly that the color drained from their lips.

The Emperor smiled and spread his hands, "Come, come my friends. Who can tell me what the sweetest music is?"

Cho Chow, a merchant, said, "The sweetest music is the sound that one of the flutes from my store makes when it is sold."

The Emperor frowned.

Chang Lo, minister of the treasury, said, "The sweetest music, I am sure you will agree, is the sound of newly minted coins jingling in your pocket."

The Emperor continued to frown.

Li Ching spoke again, "The sweetest of all music is not the sound of the flute, nor the jingling of money, but the blaring of battle horns and the clanging of swords."

Still, the Emperor frowned.

3

Other guests then shouted out, "The sweetest music is the rustle of a silk gown," or "The sound of a jewelry box opening," or "The last hammer fall driving the last nail into a new mansion."

The Emperor squinted at his guests and stood up. Everyone fell silent. The Emperor then said, "I have a place where you can think about your answers."

The Emperor's guards escorted the guests, who were stunned into silence, to the dungeon.

For three days the guests languished behind bars and slept on beds of bug-infested straw. They were given no food and only three cups of water per day.

On the first day, the Emperor visited his guests and asked, "Do you know what the sweetest music is?"

No one answered for fear of a worse fate.

On the second day, the Emperor visited his guests and asked the same question. Still, no one answered.

When the Emperor visited his guests on the third day, he noticed that they trembled and their mouths hung open. Again the Emperor asked, "What is the sweetest music?"

No one answered.

The Emperor then held out his hands. The guests gasped. In one of the Emperor's hands was a small bowl of plain rice, in the other a pair of simple wooden chopsticks. Three times the Emperor tapped the chopsticks against the side of the clay bowl.

All of the guests drooled and licked their lips. Their eyes widened with a hunger they had never known before, a hunger so deep that it felt as if their stomachs had suddenly grown teeth.

The Emperor looked at each of his guests, shook his head and said, "Do you know what the sweetest music is? It is the sound of chopsticks striking a bowl of rice in the ears of hunger—this is the sweetest music."

Whole-Language Activities for "The Hunger for Music"

Before Reading Activities

Evaluation (p. 7)

So that the students gain a greater understanding of the thematic motifs of the story, it is important that they involve themselves with them. This activity allows students to evaluate their own perceptions by ranking what they think are the most important tangible and intangible items on the list.

Further understanding occurs as the students define their criteria for ranking the items as they did. As they read the story, the students should bear in mind the importance the items have both for themselves and for the characters.

Making predictions (p. 8)

This activity sheet is designed to help students develop the thinking skills of fluency and flexibility by working with certain of the contents of the story they are to read.

After the students answer each of the questions, encourage them to share their answers so that they may see the different ways that each of them think and process information.

Vocabulary development (p. 9)

This activity sheet allows students to understand how inferences are made.

1. After all the students have written down what they think the word in italics means, have them share their answers and write down many of them on the chalkboard or on the overhead projector.

2. After the students have shared their guesses, have them look up the words

and compare the dictionary definitions with their own guesses.

During Reading Activity

Brainstorming & predicting

1. As the story is being read aloud, stop after the section in which the guests have unsuccessfully answered the emperor's question, "What is the sweetest music?"

2. Have the students brainstorm other possible answers to the emperor's question.

3. Make a list of the answers, then continue reading to see if any of the students were able to give an answer that would have pleased the emperor.

After Reading Activities

Descriptive writing (p. 10)

This activity will help students to understand the necessity and purpose for the use of specific sensory details in descriptive writing.

1. On the activity sheet are listed some aspects of the emperor's dungeon. Go over these with the students and then encourage them to add more details to the list.

2. The students should then choose at least five items from the list to use as the details in their own descriptive paragraph. The students should also use a topic sentence that is focused on one overall dominant impression. The details in their paragraphs should be clearly arranged to develop that overall impression.

Pattern writing (p. 11)

This writing pattern allows the students to develop the thinking skills of fluency, flexibility, and originality as well as help them learn to understand parallel structure.

1. You might begin by having the students think of at least ten ideas for each section of the writing pattern and then pick the best three ideas to put in the pattern.

   Note: This pattern also allows students to exercise their imaginations because each student can fill in the blanks with original ideas.

2. Before the students share their writing, they might check and be sure they have used parallel structure in each section of the pattern.   For example, in the second section, "I would spend my days..." each blank line might begin with an -ing word: I would spend my days *riding through the country-side*, *sitting on my golden throne*, and *eating expensive and exotic foods*.

3. Each section of the writing pattern should be constructed so that the language units are grammatically correct and are structured in a parallel fashion— this can be done with gerund phrases, infinitive phrases, prepositional phrases, participle phrases, etc.

EVALUATION

Rank the following in order of importance.

$100,000

Dinner with the President of the U.S.A.

Honesty

A closet full of expensive new clothes

Loyalty

A million dollar mansion

Being made a four-star general in the Army

Friendship

Wisdom

Greed

Owning your own successful business

Music

Food

Gratitude

Becoming an emperor of a vast empire

Explain how you ranked your first three choices.

Explain how you ranked your last three choices.

What else should be added to the list?

Read "Hunger for Music" and decide in what order the items should
be ranked if taken from the Emperor's point of view.

MAKING PREDICTIONS

> ### An Imperial Invitation
>
> On this first day of the ninth month in the year of the Dragon, his royal highness, Emperor Po, hereby invites you to join him for an imperial banquet where the most exotic of foods will be served for your repast and enjoyment. In addition to offering you the feast the Emperor wishes to announce that he will also treat you to a most unusual form of entertainment. Please be kind enough to inform the Emperor whether you will be in attendance.

What is the most unusual food you have ever eaten?

Make a list of the most exotic foods you can think of.

Of your exotic foods, which have you eaten? Which would you like to try? Which would you prefer not to try?

Make a list of reason why you should attend the Emperor's banquet.

Make a list of reasons why you should not attend the banquet.

The invitation says that the Emperor has planned "a most unusual form of entertainment." What could that possibly mean?

Before you read "The Hunger for Music," list all the possible ways in which a person can hunger for music.

VOCABULARY DEVELOPMENT

In each sentence, decide what you think each *italicized* word means and write down your answer:

1. For three days the guests *languished* behind bars and slept on beds of bug-infested straw.

    Your answer:

2. As the Emperor watched his guests arrive, he noticed that they were all *arrayed* in silk garments that shimmered like the wings of butterflies and wore jewels larger than birds' eggs.

    Your answer:

3. Even the rich and *pungent* aromas failed to tickle their noses.

    Your answer:

4. A feeling of hummingbirds *fluttered* in each of the guests' stomachs.

    Your answer:

5. The sweetest music is the *rustle* of a silk gown.

    Your answer:

6. Every one of the guests *drooled* and licked his lips.

    Your answer:

Now compare your answers with those in the dictionary.

DESCRIPTIVE WRITING

Here is a partial list of descriptive objects that might be found in the dungeon where the Emperor's guests languished for three days.

rusty iron bars
jagged stone walls
corners festooned with spiders' webs
the dank smell of mold
flickering torches spewing smoke
moth-eaten blankets
rats scurrying from cell to cell
the sporadic laughter of the guards
stale air
flat and lifeless straw bed
** add five more of your own:

_____

_____

_____

_____

_____

Use at least five of the details from the list in a descriptive paragraph about the dungeon:

Start with a clear topic sentence:

The dungeon was a_____place.
(fill in the blank with one word that describes what you wish to emphasize about the dungeon: *dirty, ugly, horrible, oppressive, spartan, cluttered, frightening*, etc.)

In the rest of the paragraph, be sure to focus on details and where those details are found. You may want to describe *the floor, the walls, the bars, the ceiling, the straw bed, the torches, the guards, the other creatures who live there*, etc. Focus on those things that you can *see, hear, touch, taste,* and *smell*.

PATTERN WRITING

THE HUNGER FOR MUSIC

If I were the Emperor of China

I would fill my palace with

_____,

_____,

and _____,

I would spend my days

_____,

_____,

and _____,

I would issue the following decrees:

_____,

_____,

and _____,

I would build a great wall in order to

_____,

_____,

and _____,

But most importantly, I would be able to

_____,

_____,

and _____.

That is what I would do if I were the Emperor of China.

THE STORY OF MICK MCCANN

FOLKTALE FROM IRELAND

Mick McCann was a roving and a wondering kind of man. He never had enough money to make his pockets jingle as he walked and he never owned enough of anything to fill his knapsack. He was also the kind of man who believed in facts, in those hard things that he could touch with his hands. He always said, "If I can't touch it, it's nonsense and a waste of time."

One winter's twilight, when the wind blew from the north with an icy edge, Mick found himself without a warm place to sleep. As he was trudging through an open field, Mick saw a small house in the distance. A light burned in the window, and smoke wafted from the chimney. Without hesitation, Mick scurried for the house.

Standing on the porch, Mick knocked twice. An old woman greeted him. She said, "What do you want?"

Mick replied, "Would you have a spare room, or a place by your fire where I might spend the night? I can't pay you, but I would be happy to chop some wood for you come morning."

The old woman looked at Mick, her clear blue yes sparkling like ancient jewels. She said, "You can stay the night here, but first you must tell me a story."

Mick hesitated, then said, "I don't know any stories. And even if I did, I wouldn't tell one."

"Suit yourself. No story, no place to sleep here," was all she said and closed the door in Mick's face.

Grumbling, kicking dirt, Mick stepped away from the house. He saw a barn nearby and decided that he would spend the night there, with or without the old woman's permission.

He went into the barn, laid down, covered himself with a pile of straw and fell asleep.

After a few hours, Mick awoke to the sound of voices. He peered from his mound of straw and saw three men. Each was at least twelve feet tall and together they were swinging a large and heavy sack tied to the ceiling of the barn over a roaring fire.

The men were arguing. "You swing the sack," said the first man whose voice sounded like branches breaking, "I swung the sack last night."

"I don't want to swing the sack," said the second man whose voice sounded like a boulder rolling down a hill, "I always have to swing the sack."

"I know who can swing the sack," said the third man whose voice sounded like rolling thunder. "Let Mick McCann swing the sack."

The third man turned to where Mick was hiding and boomed, "Mick McCann, Mick McCann, come out of there and swing this sack of gold!"

Trembling, Mick walked over to the three tall men. The third man said, "Mick McCann, you swing this sack of gold over this fire. But don't you let the rope break or then we will swing you over the fire!"

The three men went outside. Mick pushed the sack back and forth, back and forth. As he pushed, he started to sweat. Suddenly, the rope holding the sack snapped and the sack crashed onto the fire. Mick nearly screamed. Frenzied, Mick threw himself out a nearby window and bolted. He ran for miles until he found a culvert on the side of a dirt road. He crawled into the culvert, covered himself with grass and leaves, and waited. He barely breathed.

Mick was about to relax when he heard heavy footsteps and the sound of something heavy being dragged. Voices followed.

"You drag the bag," said the first voice. "I dragged the bag last night."

"I don't want to drag the bag," said the second voice. "I always drag the bag."

"I know who we can get to drag the bag," said the third voice. "Let's get Mick McCann to drag the bag."

The tallest of the three men walked to the edge of the culvert and boomed, "Mick McCann, Mick McCann come out of that culvert and drag this bag."

Eyes wide with fear, Mick stumbled onto the road. He took the bag and began dragging it.

"You drag that bag well," said the third man, "or else we will drag you!"

After an hour of bag dragging, Mick and the three men came to the edge of a forest. There they left Mick and stepped into the thick of trees. Mick, fearing they would come back soon, climbed up a nearby oak tree. From his position, he saw the men step out of the woods. Each was carrying a shovel. Again, they argued.

"You dig the hole," said the first man. "I dug the hole last night."

"I don't want to dig the hole," said the second man. "I always dig the hole."

"I know who we can get to dig the hole," said the third man. "Let's get Mick McCann to dig the hole."

The third man looked up at Mick perched in the oak tree and boomed, "Mick McCann, Mick McCann come down from there and dig this hole!"

Mick's face was as white as the moon that shown overhead. He climbed down and took one of the shovels.

"Dig the hole well," said the third man, "or else we will be putting you in it along with the gold."

Mick sunk the shovel into the hard earth. He dug and dug and dug. The moon began to wane. As he finished digging, Mick looked up in time to see the first rays of the sun burst like ribbons over the horizon. As he climbed out of the hole he was amazed when he saw the three men and the bag of gold vanish into thin air. His eyes twitched and his lip quivered. Mick dropped the shovel, picked up his knapsack and ran as fast and as furiously as his legs would carry him. It is said that Mick McCann ran so fast that he passed rabbits that were running along the way.

When Mick reached the town of Donborough, he felt safe. He found a bench and plopped down to rest. His breathing was just returning to normal when he heard a booming voice, "Mick McCann, Mick McCann, stand up Mick McCann!"

Mick's knees shook and then buckled as he tried to stand. His heart pounded like thunder trapped in his chest. Even the hair on the back of his neck was standing on end. Coming towards him were the three twelve-foot tall men.

When they reached him, the tallest of the three stepped up to Mick, reached down and picked him up by the shirt collar. Mick dangled in the tall man's hands like a doll.

The tall man boomed, "Now Mick McCann I've got you again. I have only one thing to tell you. The next time an old woman wants to hear a story, you tell her one!"

The man put Mick down and walked away with the other two men. Mick never saw them again.

But you wouldn't know it to hear Mick tell the story...

Whole-Language Activities for "The Story of Mick McCann"

Before Reading Activities

Expecting the unexpected (p. 17)

This activity sheet will help students learn to evaluate their own responses to difficult questions, build paragraphs and make predictions towards a literary text.

1. One effective way to use the "Warm Up for Thinking" is to make a transparency of the activity sheet to use on an overhead projector. Use a piece paper to cover all the questions but the first one. Let the students think about the choices and then write their answer down on paper.

2. After all the students have written down their responses, proceed to the next question. This technique will keep all the students focused and will also engender anticipation about the next comparisons.

3. After the students have answered all of the questions, they should choose one of them to use as the basis for a paragraph. The answer to the question will become the topic sentence and the students should think of three reasons to support their choice and one idea to use as a conclusion.

4. Finally, the students should make predictions as to which of their answers will appear in "The Story of Mick McCann."

Clustering (p. 18)

Students should use this activity sheet as a way of generating ideas based on their own perceptions and experiences.

Since the bag of gold is the central physical motif in "The Story of Mick McCann," the cluster that each student generates will serve as a bridge into the story.

Writing proverbs (p. 19)

One activity that will help students to develop language flexibility is completing open-ended sentences.

1. The students first read the proverbs at the top of the activity sheet and then try to think of more that they have heard.

2. Using those as models, students should then complete the ten sentences on the second half of the page. These completed sentences might then be shared in groups or with the entire class.

3. The students should then be informed that the ideas about which they are writing are central to "The Story of Mick McCann." As they read the story, the students should pay close attention to see how/if their sentences, or their "new proverbs," apply.

During Reading Activities

Reading for answers

The students might answer the following questions during the reading of the story.

Note: It is effective to encourage students to give many responses to the questions since there is no one correct answer for each.

Why is it so important that the old woman hear a story?

What are some reasons why Mick refuses? If you were in Mick's place, would you tell a story? If so, what?

Who are the three tall men? Where do they come from?

How do they know where Mick is each time?

Think of five words that describe Mick at the beginning and middle of the story.

Why do the men suddenly vanish?

What does the last line of the story mean?

After Reading Activities

Inferential thinking (p. 20)

One way to arrive at a better understanding of character motivation is by using inferential thinking—that is by thinking of things that would somehow be logically associated with a character.

1. Students should choose one answer from each of the four answers given for questions 1 - 10 on the activity sheet. For each answer the students should write a few sentences which justify their choices based on direct evidence from the story.

2. Students might then debate their answers, arguing their points of view from different perspectives.

Clustering / Writing a personal narrative (pp. 21-22)

This activity is divided into four steps that will take the students through the writing process. This process will allow the students to explore, shape and use language in an organized manner to write about a strange or unexpected event in their own lives.

Note: The purpose of the activity is to show the students that stories like Mick McCann are not as bizarre or as isolated as they may at first think, that with a little time to think and reflect, students see that they too have experienced something unexpected.

1. The students should follow the directions given for each step. In some ways, the most important step is *Step One* because in this step students will generate the material about which they will write. If the material they generate is neither sufficient nor detailed enough, then the narrative that follows will most likely be too general and not charged with narrative energy.

2. *Step Two* helps the students focus their writing into a manageable whole by showing them how to break the narrative action into a series of related sequences. It also introduces them to the idea of how to write a controlling statement which will facilitate a better method of organization for their narrative.

3/4. *Steps Three and Four* help the student to edit and revise both the developmental and mechanical aspects of their writing.

Responding to Before Reading Activities

Apply the Before Reading Activities to the story by having the students answer the questions in the Warm Up for Thinking from the point of view of Mick McCann.

How would Mick McCann cluster his ideas around "a bag of gold?"

How would Mick McCann finish each of the open-ended sentences on the Writing Proverbs page?

EXPECTING THE UNEXPECTED

"Warming Up for Thinking"

Which is more valuable:

> a good story or a bag of gold?

Which is more frightening:

> being lost and alone in the middle of nowhere on a
> winter night or being grabbed by a giant?

Which is a safer place in which to hide:

> a culvert of an oak tree?

Which causes more damage:

> a 60 mph freezing wind or loneliness?

Which is easier to hear:

> "Go away!" or "Now I've got you!"

Which is safer:

> hiding under a bed of straw in an isolated barn or running
> across a moonlit open field?

Which is more remarkable:

> being captured by three giants or escaping from three giants?

Which is heavier:

> a hard heart or a bag of gold?

Which is more enjoyable:

> listening to a good story or telling a good story?

Discuss each of your answers with a partner. Be sure to give reasons why you made the choices you made.

Choose one of your answers and write a paragraph which explains your choice. You might start with something like: Hiding in an oak tree would probably be safer than hiding in a culvert for the following reasons.

(reason #1)_____

(reason #2)_____

(reason #3)_____

As you read "The Story of Mick McCann," keep in mind the choices you made. After you have finished the story, decide which choices Mick would have made. How do your choices compare to the ones you think Mick would have chosen?

CLUSTERING

THE STORY OF MICK MCCANN

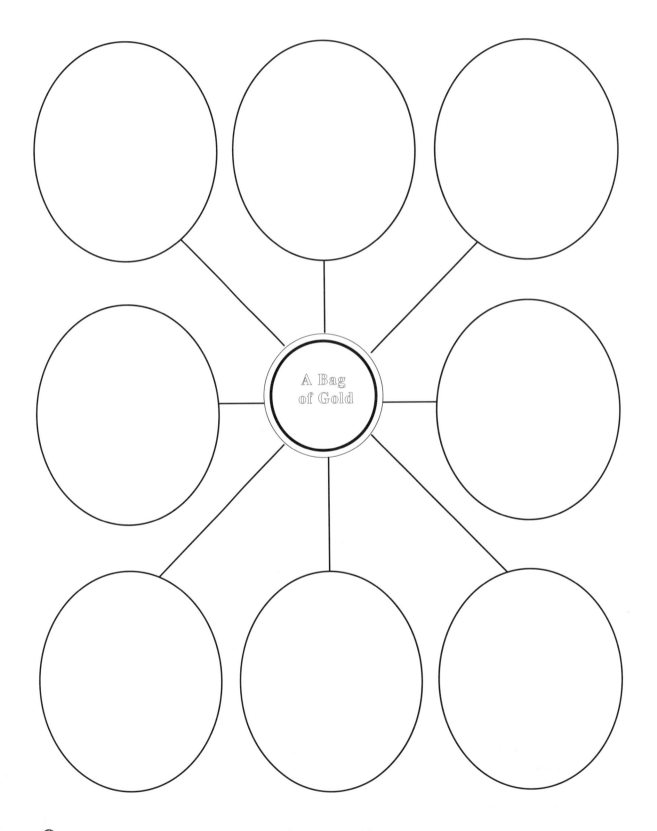

WRITING PROVERBS

THE STORY OF MICK MCCANN

Everyone is familiar with at least a few proverbs, those wise and witty folk sayings that reveal certain truths about life. For example:

> Every dark cloud has a silver lining.
> Don't count your chickens before they're are hatched.
> People who live in glass houses shouldn't throw stones.
> Good things come to those who wait.
> He who hesitates is lost.

Using these starter phrases, compose your own original proverbs.

1. Hang a bag of gold over a fire and _____

    _____.

2. Better to be captured by three giants than _____

    _____.

3. Never refuse an old woman a story _____

    _____.

4. A quiet barn _____

    _____.

5. Sleep in your own straw _____

    _____.

6. A culvert is a place in which to hide _____

    _____.

7. Avoid the forest on a winter's night _____

    _____.

8. A shovel in the hand is worth _____

    _____.

9. Don't dig a hole _____

    _____.

10. Avoid tall strangers _____

    _____.

Now read "The Story of Mick McCann." You may be surprised to discover that some of your proverbs might apply to the story.

INFERENTIAL THINKING

Choose the one answer that you think best answers the question. For this activity, there is no one correct answer as long as you can explain your choice by using evidence from "The Story of Mick McCann."

1. Mick McCann's favorite subject in school probably was:
   a. English
   b. math
   c. science
   d. history

2. Mick McCann's favorite movie would probably be:
   a. *Fantasia*
   b. *The Sound of Music*
   c. *Top Gun*
   d. *Gone With the Wind*

3. If Mick got lost in a large city, he would probably:
   a. Ask a stranger for help
   b. Try and find a city map
   c. Find a tourist information center
   d. Just keep wandering

4. If Mick had something stolen from him, he would probably:
   a. Go after the thief himself
   b. Dial 911
   c. Not give it a second thought
   d. Go to the Salvation Army for help

5. If Mick had enough money to buy a car, he would buy:
   a. a Mercedes Benz
   b. a beat-up 1963 Ford pickup truck
   c. a Chevrolet Corvette Stingray
   d. a Jeep

6. If Mick were to get a job, he would probably be a:
   a. sports reporter
   b. janitor in an office building
   c. rock musician
   d. dentist

7. Mick's favorite food would probably be:
   a. pizza
   b. steak and potatoes
   c. pancakes
   d. a foot-long hotdog

8. Mick's favorite ride at a carnival would probably be:
   a. the roller coaster
   b. the ferris wheel
   c. the bumper cars
   d. the water slide

9. Mick's favorite pet would probably be:
   a. a German Shepard
   b. a Persian cat
   c. an alligator
   d. a parrot

10. Mick's leisure time activity would probably be:
    a. hiking & backpacking
    b. watching TV
    c. reading
    d. skydiving

CLUSTERING

THE STORY OF MICK MCCANN

Cluster some ideas together as a way of writing about an unexpected incident in your own life.

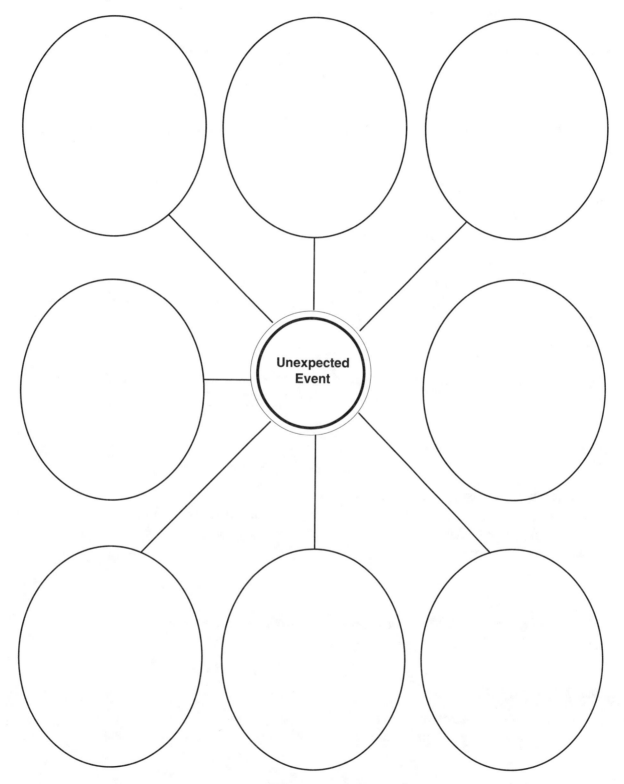

WRITING A PERSONAL NARRATIVE

Step One: Gathering ideas

Use the cluster chart to gather ideas about an unexpected event that you experienced in your own life. An unexpected event can be pleasant, for example, like the time you hit a grand slam home run or found a $5 bill on the sidewalk. An unexpected event can be unpleasant, for example, the time you ripped your new pants at school, or the time you sat on your own lunch, twice. An unexpected event can also be weird, for example, the time you got your head stuck between the railings of the stairway in your house, or the time that you only got half a hair cut.

Step Two: Organizing and writing

Now that you have generated some ideas, you might want to put them together so that a reader can easily follow your story. Answer the following questions to help with the organization and focus of your writing:

1. Exactly where did the event take place?

2. How old were you?

3. Who else, if anyone, was involved?

4. How long did the event last?

5. What objects were involved?

6. Was anything important spoken by either yourself or anyone else? What?

7. Plot the sequence of events on the chart below.

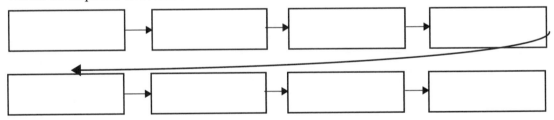

You might begin your personal narrative with something like:

One day when I was____years old, something unexpected happened to me.

(Set the scene, give background information and introduce any other people who were involved. Continue the narrative by developing the action and the resulting chain of events that occurred. Be sure to describe your reactions to the situation as well.)

Step Three: Editing

Check your writing for: a clear focus and sense of organization, sentence structure, word choice, spelling and punctuation.

Step Four: Final draft

Make a final draft of your work. Share it with a classmate. Perhaps your class will want to make a book of narratives in which everyone contributes a chapter.

GOLDEN SILENCE

FOLKTALE FROM AFGHANISTAN

Characters: Narrator, thief, jailkeeper, king, queen, judge, general, chief of police, thief's wife.

Narrator: Early one morning at the town bazaar a man was caught stealing a jar of olive oil by the chief of police. The chief of police brought the thief before the judge.

Judge: What happened?

Chief: I caught this man stealing a jar of olive oil.

Judge: (*to the thief*) How do you plead?

Thief: Alas, it is true, Your Honor. I took the jar of olive oil because I have no money and my wife needs the oil.

Judge: Very well. Either pay the fine or spend two years in jail.

Thief: As I said, Your Honor, I have no money.

Narrator: The thief was taken to the jailkeeper who threw him into a jail cell. Just as the gate slammed shut, the thief cried out.

Thief: Jailkeeper, take me to the king!

Jailkeeper: You are crazy. Why should I take you to the king?

Thief: Tell him I have a gift of great value.

Jailkeeper: You must think me a fool. The king would have my head if I disturbed him.

Thief: The king will have your head if he finds out that you didn't take me to him, especially when he finds out what it is I have to offer him. But make up your own mind. If you think it is best that I stay here...

Jailkeeper: All right! All right, I'll take you to the king. But you had better be telling the truth!

Narrator: The thief was taken to the king. When the thief entered the king's throne room, he noticed that the queen, the general, the chief of police, the judge and the jailkeeper were all present.

King: This jailkeeper tells me you have something of extraordinary value for me.

Thief: Yes, Your Highness.

King: Well, what is it? Do you think I have time to waste with someone like you?

Thief: It is this, an olive pit.

Narrator: The thief took an olive pit from his picket and handed it to the king.

King: An olive pit? Do you mock me?

Thief: Oh, no, Your Highness. You see, if you plant this olive pit, the olive tree that springs from it will yield nothing but golden olives.

King: So you say. If what you say is true, why haven't you planted this olive pit?

Thief: Only someone who has never stolen, cheated or lied can plant the olive pit and reap golden olives. If a dishonest person planted the pit, the tree that grew would be poisonous. That is why I want you to have the olive pit, Your Highness, because surely you have never stolen, cheated or lied in your life.

Narrator: The king was silent, remembering the time when he had cheated some land away from the king of the neighboring kingdom.

King: You are very kind, thief, but I cold not accept such a gift. Perhaps the queen would like it instead.

Narrator: The queen blushed as she remembered the time she had stolen beauty secrets from a queen in a neighboring country who had been visiting.

Queen: Oh, no thank you. The olive pit is surely not for me. Perhaps the general can benefit from it.

Narrator: The general gulped hard, remembering the times he had cheated to get promotions in the king's army.

General: I couldn't possibly accept such a gift. No, perhaps the judge would like the olive pit.

Narrator: The judge grew pale. His hands trembled as he remembered the time he had accepted a large bribe to let a guilty bandit go free.

Judge: Me? *No*, no. No, thank you. *No*, not at all. I know, perhaps the chief of police would like to have the olive pit.

Narrator: The chief's eyes widened. Sweat beaded on his forehead as he remembered the time he had stolen part of his officers' payroll to pay for his own gambling expenses.

Chief: Well, perhaps, I could take… but on second thought, no. I could not possibly accept the olive pit. Perhaps the jailkeeper could take it.

Narrator: The jailkeeper shifted from foot to foot. He scratched his head as he remembered the times he had taken money from the prisoners in exchange for better food.

Jailkeeper: I must decline the olive pit. It is not for me.

Thief: Will no one take this magic, golden olive pit? Surely one of you would be happy to take it?

King: No, not I.

Queen: Nor I.

General: Nor I.

Judge: Nor I.

Chief: Nor I.

Jailkeeper: Nor I.

Thief: Well, I suppose then that I must return to my jail cell and stay there for the next two years because I do admit to stealing a jar of olive oil.

Narrator: As the jailkeeper led the thief out of the throne room the king suddenly called.

King: Wait! Bring that man back here.

Jailkeeper: Yes, Your Highness.

King: Thief, I have something to say to you.

Thief: What is it, Your Highness?

King: Perhaps I have been too hasty with you. After thinking about this matter, I have decided that all of us here should pay your fine for stealing the jar of olive oil. For if the truth be known, I suspect that all of us have at one time or another done something that was not honest. Go now, thief. You have shown us things about ourselves that we had chosen to ignore. For this we thank you. And one more thing, take this with you.

Narrator: The king handed the thief a jar of olive oil. The thief left the palace and later met his wife at home.

Wife: You were gone so long that I had begun to worry about. Are you all right?

Thief: I am fine, a little amazed, but fine just the same.

Wife: Well, did you get the jar of olive oil that I asked you to get?

Thief: Oh yes, here it is, but you'll never believe me when I tell you how I got it!

Whole-Language Activities for "Golden Silence"

Before Reading Activities

Analysis and evaluation (p. 28)

In the story "Golden Silence," each character has done something that he/she would rather not admit—and this is the central motif upon which the story is built. This activity sheet gives students the opportunity to place themselves in hypothetical situations that are based upon acting honestly or dishonestly.

1. Assign students to each situation, either alone or in groups, and have them decide what they would do.

2. A follow up discussion as to why the students made the choices they did will be effective. Students should then rank the ten situations from most serious to least serious.

3. Ask them to share their choices and their criteria.

Fluent and flexible thinking (p. 29)

1. Have students brainstorm about different uses for a single olive pit.

   Note: All answers should be accepted no matter how convergent or how divergent. Encourage "piggy-backing," that is, using one response as a springboard for other responses.

2. Based on the uses they have generated, allow them to answer question 2 on the activity sheet. This activity will encourage creative thinking and will also serve as a bridge to the story. Also, ask students to predict what the thief does to get out of jail.

Oral inflection (p. 30)

Students will discover how different vocal inflections can change the meaning of a sentence when read aloud.

1. Students should read aloud each of the ten sentences on the activity sheet and decide exactly what each sentence means.

2. Now have students practice reading the question, "You have been accused of stealing a jar of olive oil, how do you plead?" in a variety of ways.

During Reading Activities

Group reading

One effective way for the reading of a short play is to break the students into groups of nine so that while each group reads the play to themselves, each student has a part.

1. Before reading their parts aloud, each student should underline words he/she wants to emphasize with oral inflection.

2. After each group has read the play, make new groups: a group of students who read the part of narrator, thief, jailkeeper, etc. The students should compare the words they underlined and discuss their reasons for doing so.

After Reading Activities

Synthesis (p. 31)

This activity sheet connects with the Before Reading Activity: Analysis and Evaluation (p.28).

1. Students should recall what each character's offence was in the play. They should

then rank those offenses from most to least serious.

2. Using the thinking process of synthesis, students should assign a punishment to the most serious offender by choosing four items from the list on the activity sheet. Students should combine the items into a punishment.

Note: There is no physical pain allowed—this will force the students to use their imaginations.

Writing pattern / Phrase etymologies *(pp. 32-33)*

This activity sheet will encourage students to explore new language patterns and the reasons why those patterns came into existence.

1. Students should brainstorm phrases that are common usage (like those on the activity sheet) and then research their origins.

2. They should use the model for Putting On The Dog as a way of reporting their findings, that is, students should write three paragraphs: one paragraph is the correct explanation for the origin of the phrase they have researched, while two paragraphs should be false (but should sound as if they could be true).

3. The students can then exchange papers and try and discover the one correct answer for each phrase.

ANALYSIS & EVALUATION

Rank the following from most powerful to least powerful:

greed   jealousy   anger   deception

revenge   loneliness   fear   dishonesty

envy   corruption

Read each of the following and decide what you would do.

1. You are in a department store with your best friend. You see your friend put an expensive pen & pencil set, a silk tie, and three silk scarves into his/her coat pocket. What will you do?

2. You are in a department store. You see someone from your school who you don't like put an expensive pen & pencil set, a self tie, and three silk scarves into his/her coat pocket. What will you do?

3. You discover that, through some kind of mix-up, you have been given a test with all the correct answers filled in. What will you do?

4. You find a teacher's edition of a text book (one with all the answers in it) for your class in the hallway. No one sees you pick it up. What will you do with it?

5. Instead of buying some groceries that you were asked to buy with your parent's money, you lost it betting on a frog-jumping contest. What will you do?

6. You are in a grocery store and see someone who you know is very poor hide a loaf of bread inside of his/her coat. What will you do?

7. Your best friend asks you to lie for him/her and tell anyone who asks that he/she was with you last night. You know for a fact that your friend is the one who let the air out of all the bus tires. What will you do?

8. A local stereo components store was broken into last night. You know who did it. In fact it is a person in your class who you neither like nor dislike. When this person is questioned by the school authorities you hear him/her lie. What will you do?

9. You overhear a group of students in your school, a group you do not like very well, plan to break into the school after everyone has left. What will you do?

10. Some acquaintances of yours ask you to help them sell phony magazine subscriptions. What will you do?

Rank these 10 situations in order of most serious to least serious. Give reasons to explain your ranking. What emotions are present in each situation? Do you think the emotions are the cause or result of the situations? Explain.

FLUENT & FLEXIBLE THINKING

1. How many different uses can you think of for a single olive pit?

_____

_____

_____

_____

2. Imagine you find yourself in an Afghanistan jail hundreds of years ago. You have been accused of stealing. You look through your pockets and discover a single olive pit. How can you use a single olive pit to free yourself from jail? Tell about it.

_____

_____

_____

_____

_____

_____

_____

_____

_____

_____

_____

_____

ORAL INFLECTION

Read each of the following aloud, emphasizing the word in *italics*.

1. *I* did not steal the jar of olive oil.

2. I did *not* steal the jar of olive oil.

3. I did not *steal* the jar of olive oil.

4. I did not steal the *jar* of olive oil.

5. I did not steal the jar of *olive* oil.

6. I did not steal the jar of olive *oil*.

7. *I* have a gift for the king.

8. I have a *gift* for the king.

9. I have a gift *for* the king.

10. I have a gift for the *king*.

Read the following sentences aloud. Underline the words you wish to emphasize.

1. You have been accused of stealing a jar of olive oil, how do you plead?

2. You have been accused of stealing a jar of olive oil, how do you plead?

3. You have been accused of stealing a jar of olive oil, how do you plead?

4. You have been accused of stealing a jar of olive oil, how do you plead?

5. You have been accused of stealing a jar of olive oil, how do you plead?

6. You have been accused of stealing a jar of olive oil, how do you plead?

Now find a partner and compare the words you each have underlined. Then read the sentences to one another.

SYNTHESIS

For each character below, list the offence that each is responsible for in "Golden Silence." Rank each character by offence: from most serious to least serious. Explain your criteria for ranking.

Thief:

King:

Queen:

Judge:

General:

Chief of Police:

Jailkeeper:

Should any punishment be meted out to the most serious offender on your list? Why/why not?

Imagine that the state demands some kind of punishment for the offender who you ranked as number one. From the items below, choose *any four* and incorporate them into the punishment—remember: No physical pain is allowed.

Items:

umbrella	old tennis shoes	empty clay jar
broken key	dull pencil	ball of yarn
melted wax	two feathers	straw mattress
a kite	the cover of a softball	baby powder
a bucket	three buttons	an apple core
a sack of onions	a mousetrap	a broom
an old calendar	a hunk of fool's gold	a wagon wheel
six dried flowers	nine firecrackers without fuses	a doll

WRITING PATTERN

Have you ever wondered where certain phrases that we use came from?
For example, are you curious about how the following phrases came into being:

This is the pits!

He sure is putting on the dog.

We're really in a pickle this time.

This makes me feel like a hog on ice.

She sure is the bee's knees.

I hate it when I have to eat humble pie.

It's raining cats and dogs.

The boss just gave him the ax.

She let the cat out of the bag.

This car can stop on a dime.

That's the way the cookie crumbles.

We're in hot water now.

We don't see eye to eye on this.

In the story, "Golden Silence," the thief probably understood the expression, "This is the pits," quite clearly. Being stuck with an olive pit and being in jail, the thief was in a position where things could not get much worse—for him, his situation was certainly "the pits."

Here is a way to investigate why phrases mean what they mean, and how they came into being. Below are three possible etymologies for the phrase, "putting on the dog." Only one etymology is correct. Can you guess which?

Putting On the Dog

1. This phrase originated in the Nordic countries circa 1700. At that time, many people travelled by dog sled from town to town and village to village. Occasionally and unexpectedly a blizzard would blow in from the north and trap a lone traveller. Because the blizzards were often severe enough to be life-threatening, a person who was suddenly caught in one had no choice but to stop, dig a shallow hole in the snow, lay in the hole, and cover himself with his sled dogs. The dogs would keep the traveller warm until the blizzard passed. Hence, the phrase (when translated into English), putting on the dog.

2. This phrase originated in the United State circa 1800. Wealthy Americans who travelled to Europe in the early nineteenth century noticed that a custom among royalty was to place small and exotic dogs on their laps when they received guests from abroad. The Americans, wanting desperately to imitate the royalty of Europe in all manner of

custom, soon started placing small and exotic dogs on their laps when they received guests from anywhere. Hence, the phrase, putting on the dog.

3. This phrase originated in England circa 1900. One important part of a fireman's work is to save people who are trapped in burning buildings. Before there was sufficient technology which allowed firemen to enter burning buildings and still be able to breath, Dalmatian dogs were used. The dogs would enter the buildings, find anyone who was trapped, and drag or lead him/her out of danger. Consequently, before firemen left the firehouse to put out a fire, they always put the dogs (Dalmatians) on their fire trucks. Hence, the phrase, putting on the dog.

(The correct answer is #2)

Choose a phrase and do some research to find out its origin. Then write three explanations of that phrase's origin: one should be the correct one, and two of them should be spurious (incorrect), but should sound like they could be correct. Exchange papers with other classmates and see if you can spot the correct phrase etymologies.

Can you think of ways in which the phrases you research may apply to the story, "Golden Silence"?

For example:

At the beginning of the story, wasn't the thief caught *red handed?*

Didn't the thief *bite off more than he could chew* before he thought of what to do with the olive pit?

Wasn't the thief's idea *a horse of a different color?*

Didn't the thief *try to beat the rap?*

Didn't the king think the thief was *off his rocker?*

How many other phrases can you apply to the characters or the plot events in the story?

GIANTS & MOSQUITOES

FOLKTALE OF THE NORTH AMERICAN INDIANS

In the days when the sky was green and the sun was pink and the moon followed a golden path in the indigo night sky, a band of fierce giants lived in the scarlet mountains. The people who lived in the valley where the lavender grass grew were deathly afraid of the giants.

Every night, as blue owls sat singing their mysterious songs in the gray trees, the people of the valley listened to the giants rumble and roar in the mountains. The people knew it was only a matter of time until the ravenous giants left the scarlet mountains and invaded the valley in search of food—human food. The people also knew the sign their grandfathers had taught them to watch for: When the blue owls stop singing in the gray trees and the moon did not appear in the night sky, beware of the giants!

One night, when the moon did not follow the golden path and the blue owls sat silently in the gray trees, the people of the valley knew that the giants were coming to devour them. They gathered in council to devise a plan to rid themselves of the giants.

A warrior spoke, "We must gather our weapons and destroy the giants."

Many people nodded with approval and the warriors moved to gather their arrows and spears.

The chief then spoke, "Wait. Do not go to make war on the giants. Do you remember the people who lived in the yellow desert?

They tried war. Even thought they fought bravely, their spears and arrows were like splinters sticking in the giants' skin and the giants devoured them all."

Another warrior spoke, "We should gather ourselves and flee this place. We will find another valley in which to live."

A woman spoke, "No. We must not leave. This is our home. This valley is the place where we are one with the earth. Go if you must go, but I will not leave."

The chief spoke again, "She is right. We are the people of the valley. We must not flee."

The shaman then said, "Perhaps there is another way. I have an idea. Last night I dreamed of giants and of the lavender grass, and I think I have found a solution. We must act swiftly, though, for the giants will be here soon."

Following the shaman's directions, the men went into the valley and gathered as much lavender grass as they could carry. The women began sewing together buffalo skins. When the men returned, they stuffed their armfuls of lavender grass into the buffalo skins that were now sewn together. When they had finished, they looked at what they had just created: lying on the ground before them was a huge man stuffed with lavender grass whose skin was made of buffalo hides. The women then dressed the stuffed man with a hurriedly sewn together set of clothes while the shaman painted a human face on the figure. Finally, the shaman sprinkled some herbs from his leather pouch over the length of the stuffed man's body.

A roar like thunder erupting from inside a great stone shattered the night. The people knew that the giants had entered the valley. Quickly the people hid themselves in holes that the shaman had directed them to dig. The holes were large enough to hide the people, but small enough so that the giants would not be able to step in them.

Growling and snorting, the giants arrived. When they discovered the stuffed man laying on the ground, the giants roared with laughter.

"Look," said one of the giants, "these people of the valley are so terrified of us that they die even before we come."

"Yes," said another, "imagine how easy it will be to eat tonight. All we have to do is wander through this valley picking up humans lying on the ground who died for fear of us! Oh yes, I like this place!"

"Wait," said a third giant, "who gets to eat this first human being?"

"I found him," said the first giant, "therefore I will eat him."

The other giants grumbled.

The second giant said, "You won't eat that human being first, I will!" He then lunged toward the first giant who had picked up the stuffed man. The second giant grappled and clawed, bellowed and growled.

The other giants then threw themselves into the fight over the stuffed man. They snarled and gouged, punched and kicked, screamed and wailed. Each giant managed to rip away a part of the stuffed man's body and hungrily devour it. As each of the giants sat down to rest, their faces, which were normally magenta, changed color and became dark purple. The giants clutched their throats, gasping for air. Their eyes bulged, and their ears began to hiss. Even their hair stood on end, becoming gray like

the surrounding trees. The giants fell backwards landing with a great crash.

The shaman crawled out of his hiding place. He walked up to the first giant who was the giant's chief and said, "You have been fooled giant. That was no human being you ate, but a bag of buffalo hides stuffed with lavender grass. I wove a spell over it, a spell that is turning you to ashes."

The giant's chief spoke, "You may turn us to ashes, but we will devour you until the end of time."

One by one the giants crumbled until there was nothing left of them but huge mounds of ashes and dust. Just then, a strong wind from the north blew out of the scarlet mountains and stirred the ashes into the air. Instantly each particle of ash turned into a mosquito. The cloud of ashes became a cloud of mosquitoes.

The shaman felt a small sting. Then he felt another sting and then another. He looked and saw three mosquitoes on his arm. He slapped them away and scratched his arm where he had been bitten, as a tiny buzzing sound rang in his ears.

Whole-Language Activities for "Giants & Mosquitoes"

Before Reading Activities

Flexible thinking (p. 38)

The story "Giants & Mosquitoes" makes use of flexible thinking in the way it uses color. This activity sheet is designed to help facilitate flexible thinking in the students. The activity sheet begins with the students' experiences and then helps them broaden their perspectives and imaginations.

1. First, students name as many colors as they can: encourage them not to stop with the primary colors but to list colors such as mauve, puce, cat's eye green, or banana yellow.

2. Then have students choose the most important color—this allows them to plug in to their own internal value systems.

3. Third, the students choose four colors and name as many things as they can that are those colors.

4. Students now use the first three steps to answer questions that promote flexible thinking: What would happen if every rain drop was a different color, etc.

5. Finally, students are to use flexible thinking to describe colors to someone who cannot see.

Vocabulary development (p. 39)

1. In this activity sheet, the students are given a copy of the opening passage from "Giants & Mosquitoes" in which the descriptive words have been replaced with blank spaces. Students then fill in the blanks with words that they think are most appropriate.

2. Based on their versions, the students should predict two things that might happen in the story. They should then compare their version with the story.

   Note: The words should be generated from the students.

During Reading Activities

After the students read the first two paragraphs of the story, ask them why unusual colors are used to describe the sky, sun, moon, mountains, grass, owls and trees. How do the colors change the story? What purpose do they serve?

Note: One idea to work towards: The story is set in a distant time, a time when magic and mysterious people and events were possible.

After Reading Activities

Analysis (p. 40)

This activity sheet is designed to help students gain a greater understanding of theme.

By choosing statements from the activity sheet which best fit the story, students will understand how to infer a general idea from a specific story.

Note: This story/activity can also be a springboard for research about giant things in today's world.

Process writing (p. 41)

1. Using the story as a model, students should then write their own explanation or creation folktale.

2. This activity sheet is broken in four steps that direct students through specific writing sequences. The activity allows for

student individuality and creativity in that each student will write something unique.

Note: Students should also be encouraged to read other explanation/creation folktales for further modeling.

FLEXIBLE THINKING

How many different answers can you think of for the following:

1. How many different colors can you name?

2. Of the colors you named, which is the *most* important one? Why? Which is the *least* important one? Why?

3. Choose any four colors and think of as many different things as you can that are those colors. Would it make a difference if the things you chose were different colors? How?

4. What would happen if:

   a. every rain drop was a different color?

   b. if the ocean was orange?

   c. if the sun was pink?

   d. if people had rainbow colored hair?

   e. if every living creature was purple?

   f. if everything in our world was gray?

   g. if the rainbow was silver?

5. Choose one color you *like* and one color you *don't like*. How would you describe those colors to someone who has never been able to see?

   Examples: florescent orange—this color makes me think of the sound a bus makes when it shifts its gears without the clutch.
   pink—this color makes me think of the sweet taste of cotton candy.

   rust—this color makes me think of how tin-foil feels between my teeth.

   lavender—this color makes me think of the sweet aroma of the lilac.

VOCABULARY DEVELOPMENT

GIANTS & MOSQUITOES

Fill in the blanks with words that you think will complete the passage.

In the days when the sky was_____and the sun

was_____and the moon followed a_____

path in the_____ sky, a band of _____

giants lived in the _____ mountains. The people who

lived in the valley where the _____ grass grew were

_____ afraid of the giants.

Every night, as _____ owls sat singing their

_____songs in the _____trees, the

people of the valley listened to the giants _____ and

_____ in the mountains. The people knew it was

only a matter of time until the _____ giants left the

mountains and_____the valley in search

of _____.

Compare your version with the opening passage of "Giants & Mosquitoes."

Based on this passage, make two predictions as to what you think will happen later in the story "Giants & Mosquitoes."

a.

b.

Before reading the story, answer this question:

What do giants and mosquitoes have in common? (*Try and think of at least ten different answers.*)

ANALYSIS

Which of the following statements best fits the story "Giants & Mosquitoes"? Explain your answer.

Which statements do not fit the story? Explain.

1. Oh, it is excellent to have a giant's strength; but it is tyrannous to use it like a giant.

2. There were giants in the earth in those days and they have not left us yet.

3. Whoever excels in what we prize, becomes a hero in our eyes.

4. We are never deceived; we deceive ourselves.

5. We are easily fooled by the one thing we want most of all.

6. It is always darkest before the storm.

7. The more things change, the more they stay the same.

8. Instead of complaining about the darkness, light a candle.

9. Every time you win, you lose a little.

10. There's a giant inside of everyone just waiting to get out.

How many giant things that actually exist can you name?

Examples: The Sears Tower in Chicago, The Arch in St. Louis, The Grand Canyon, The Great Wall of china, a redwood tree, etc.

From your list, choose any three. Research them in your library. What do they all have in common?

Choose one thing from your list that was created by man. How was it created? Why was it created? What special problems had to be overcome in its construction? How long do you think the structure will last?

PROCESS WRITING

GIANTS & MOSQUITOES

Step One: Getting started

One important aspect of "Giants & Mosquitoes" is it tells how mosquitoes were created. Choose something you've wondered about, something that interests you or something that you think might be enjoyable to write about to use as the basis for your own creation folktale.

For example, you might want to write about how cats got their tails, or how the sun came into being, or why the moon disappears once a month, or why giraffes have long necks, or why there is dew on the grass in the summer, or why dogs bark instead of chirp, or why wheels are round, or why penguins can't fly, or why trees grow vertically instead of horizontally, or why people have language and animals don't, etc.

Step Two: Writing

One thing that many creation stories have in common is that the thing being created is often done as a solution (either wanted or unwanted) to a problem.

Another motif that creation stories share is that the thing created is often the result of foolishness on the part of either the creator or itself. (Example: Frogs have no tails because of a mistake they made when they tried to deceive the Great Spirit.)

Choose the motif you would like to work with, create a setting, choose characters and identify the problem that exists.

Remember: The way the problem in your story is resolved should somehow influence the creation idea you are describing.

Step Three: Editing

Check your writing to make sure that your story moves clearly from beginning to end with no gaps in thought. Does the way the creation idea in your story comes about make sense? (It can be magical or fantastic, but still must make sense within the framework of your story.)

Step Four: Final draft

Read your story aloud. Is it too short? Too long? Do your sentences flow smoothly? Do you have vivid verbs, nouns and adjectives? Do you surprise the listener?

JEWELS AND RAVENS

FOLKTALE FROM AFRICA

At the foot of Mt. Kilimanjaro lived an old couple. The man had a disposition like summer itself; he was warm, generous and kind. Anything he touched on his farm blossomed and flowered into beauty or flourished to produce a bounty for harvest. Because the man had a warm heart, he made it a habit of inviting his relatives, friends, and even strangers into his house for a meal and a cool drink of spring water.

The man's generosity, however, greatly angered his wife. She was a woman whose breath blew with the glacial wind of winter. Her hands were like ice, fastening on anything she touched with a numbing cold. Her eyes were so cold that she could stare a sudden chill into any living thing.

Late one summer afternoon the husband, who was weeding his vegetable garden, heard a terrible commotion in the sky. He looked up to see a small white dove dodging and darting in jagged arcs, desperately trying to avoid the clutches of a large black raven. The dove shrieked once as the raven's outstretched talons clipped one of its wings. Like a feathery comet, the dove tumbled from the sky and landed with a thud at the man's feet. The raven dove after the wounded bird, but the man brandished his hoe and drove the raven away. The man then gently lifted the dove and carried it into his house where he set to mending its broken wing.

When the mans' wife saw him she said, "What are you doing with that stupid bird?"

The man replied, "It has been hurt. We must nurse it back to health."

The wife said, "I think we should boil it in some soup. It would taste very good for supper."

The man said, "You leave this bird alone. You are not to touch it."

The wife grumbled and went outside.

The man placed the dove in a small wooden cage. He then went outside and resumed his work in the garden.

Every day the dove grew stronger. The man spent many hours with it, holding it cupped in his hands like in a nest, or softly singing to it as it sat on his shoulder. Whenever the man's wife entered the room and threw the dove an icy stare, the bird trembled.

After many weeks the dove's wing was almost completely healed and the man knew that it would soon be time to set the bird free. He was saddened by this because the dove had become a source of joy to him.

One day, after the man had gone into a nearby town to sell some of his vegetables, the wife skulked over to the dove's cage, quietly opened the door and grabbed the bird with her icy fingers. The dove shrieked, pecking and clawing at the hand that held it. The wife was so startled at this that she relaxed her grip for an instant. The dove flew from her hand. The wife grabbed a broom and chased the terrified dove around the room. The wife slashed and hacked at the bird with such force that she accidentally smashed the broom into her kitchen cabinet. Dishes shattered and flew in a thousand pieces across the room. The womans' face brightened like white ice with fury. She renewed her attack on the bird and with one last desperate slash struck the bird just as it was escaping through an open window. The dove screeched once, tumbled end over end, managed to find its wings again and flew away from the house.

"Good riddance!" said the wife, who did not know that she had struck the dove with such force that she had blinded the poor bird.

When the husband returned, he saw the cage was empty. He asked his wife, who was cleaning up the broken dishes, what had happened. When his wife told him the story the man's face grew as dark as a summer storm. He said nothing to his wife but hurried into the forest, whistling and calling for the dove. He searched through the night but found nothing.

With the approach of dawn the man found himself standing near a gate which led into a beautiful garden. The man entered and discovered a beautiful young woman who was sitting among flowers, quietly singing. Without looking up she said, "Who is there?"

The man spoke, "Excuse me, but I am looking for a dove. I know it sounds silly, but I nursed the bird back to health after it had been attacked by a raven."

Tears dropped from the young woman's eyes. She turned towards the man and said, "I am the dove that you saved from the raven."

The man gasped as he saw that her eyes were colorless and sightless. "What has happened to you?" he asked.

"I have lost my sight," she replied, "but never mind that. Here, sit and rest. I will bring you food and cool water."

The man ate and the young woman sat beside him and sang songs that were as soft as moonlight. The man stayed until dusk. As he was about to leave, the young woman said, "You must come and visit me once every month. But before you go let me give you a gift."

She set three wooden chests before him and said, "Choose any one of them."

The man thought for moment, and then picked up the smallest, put it in his pocket and said, "I will return in a month's time," and walked home.

It was pitch dark when the man returned home. His wife greeted him with, "Did you find your silly bird? and Why have you been gone so long?"

The man said nothing but put the small wooden chest on the table. His wife opened it. As she looked inside her eyes grew as large as ostrich eggs. Sitting in the chest was a diamond the size of a baby dove. It looked like a tiny star.

The wife grasped the diamond, turned to her husband and screamed, "Tell me where you got this! Tell me! Tell me! Tell me! If you don't, I will make your life so miserable that you will wish you were dead."

Hesitantly, the husband told his wife about the garden in the forest. His wife bolted from the house and nearly flew into the forest.

After many hours, the wife found the garden. Her face was drawn and haggard, her hair snarled and tangled. She stomped past the gate, found the young woman and said to her, "You gave my husband this diamond. But it is not enough. I want you to offer me the two other treasure chests that you offered him. And I want it now!"

The young woman said, "If that is what you wish, follow me."

She led the wife to the end of the garden where flowers were dying and where small plants turned brown from lack of water. Here she placed two wooden chests before the wife and said, "You may choose one of these."

The wife grabbed the larger of the two and picked it up. It was so large that she almost could not carry it. As she made her way home, she stumbled and fell many times beneath the weight of the chest. When she reached home, her clothes were torn, her knees were bleeding from scrapes, and her face was bruised and cut. She set the chest down on the table and said to her husband, "You are a fool to have chosen the smallest one. Now we will be rich beyond our dreams."

The wife grabbed hold of the lid and yanked it open. As she looked inside her mouth gaped open and all color drained from her face. Instead of jewels, a host of ravens sat squawking in the chest. The wife gasped. The ravens flew like an angry cloud out of the chest and attacked the wife. Seeing this, the husband grabbed the broom and knocked them from his wife. He then smashed and slapped at the ravens until he had swept them out of the house. When he entered the house again, he discovered that even though his wife was alive, the ravens had pecked out her eyes.

The husband helped his wife to bed where he said, "I must take care of you and mend you back to health."

After many months, the wife did return to health, and many people will tell you that she is now much kinder than she used to be.

Whole-Language Activities for "Jewels and Ravens"

Before Reading Activities

Analysis and evaluation (p. 47)

1. This activity incorporates the students' experiences into both generative and critical thinking. Students are given the opportunity to create the perfect friend by choosing five components from the list of items on the activity sheet. Since the students can only choose five items from the list, they must establish criteria for the traits they feel a good friend should possess.

2. Once the students have chosen their items and have established their criteria, they should then defend their choices with three reasons per choice.

   Note: By following the writing model on the activity sheet, the students will learn how to structure argumentative paragraphs.

Plus and minus (p. 48)

Students will discover through this activity that positive events also can have a down side.

Using the examples on the activity sheet as models, students should examine the ten positive situations and think of as many different "down sides" for them as they can.

Note: This will encourage flexible thinking and will also serve as a bridge from the students' experience to the story, "Jewels and Ravens."

During Reading Activities

Descriptive details

1. Read aloud only the first paragraph of the story.

2. Ask the students to list other physical details that might describe the old woman: encourage them to offer specific sensory images.

3. Do the same for the last two paragraphs of the story. Ask the students to list physical details that describe the old woman.

4. Now have the students compare their lists.

After Reading Activities

Analysis and evaluation (p. 49)

In order to understand that an important element of folktales is to see how and why characters change, students should complete the accompanying activity sheet.

1. Arrange the students in groups of two or three and let them discuss which values best describe each character.

   Note: The students should use evidence from the story to support their choices.

2. Students should then decide which values change during the story for each character. They should support their choices with evidence from the story.

Pattern writing / Poetry (p. 50-52)

Through this activity sheet, students can exercise their imaginations and project themselves into the future. They should decide what kind of person they might become by the time they have reached "old age."

1. First, students make a list of activities that they enjoy doing today.

2. Students should then list activities that they think they will enjoy doing when they are much older.

   Note: Encourage students to think of divergent activities for their second list.

3. Finally, students should insert various specific activities into the writing pattern that follows.

ANALYSIS AND EVALUATION

Imagine that you have been given the opportunity to create your own friend, someone who could be everything you wanted him/her to be. Of the list below, choose *five* that you would want a friend to be or to have:

good looks	rancor	a new car	athletic skills
honesty	lots of money	greed	tons of clothes
sincerity	popularity	trustworthy	calm disposition
witty	charm	moody	gloomy outlook
intelligence	generous	luck	free concert tickets
famous friends	shyness	courage	free airline tickets
no patience	stubbornness	great jokes	follows rules
wild	belligerence	awesome stereo	vacation house in Florida

Rank your five choices in order of importance. Use one of your five choices to complete this writing pattern:

My ideal friend would have (or be)_____ for three reasons.

Reason # 1:

Reason # 2:

Reason # 3:

Example: My ideal friend would be generous for three reasons.

Reason # 1: Generosity is important in a friendship because a friend will give time to you when you need to talk about what's on your mind.

Reason # 2: Generosity is important in a friendship because a friend will give you the benefit of the doubt if you make a mistake.

Reason # 3: Generosity is important in a friendship because a friend will sometimes give you special gifts that wouldn't mean as much if they came from someone else.

PLUS AND MINUS

Make a list of things that you think people want most in life. Share your lists. What is the *one* thing that you, as a class, think people want most in life? Why?

Did you ever get something that you had dreamed of getting only to discover that you got more than you bargained for?

Examples:

You have begged your mother to buy you a dress that you saw advertised in a magazine. You thought that if you had that dress, you would be happy forever. Your mother surprises you for your birthday with the dress of your dreams. You rush to your room to try it on. As you zip it up, the dress rips apart in your hands.

You have just been made quarterback of the school football team. It is something that you have wanted ever since you were old enough to throw a football. On the first play of your first game, you are tackled so hard that you sprain your ankle and knee, and must miss the rest of the season.

How many "down sides" can you think of for each of the following situations?

1. You get the car of your dreams.

2. You win a $5 million lottery.

3. You meet someone you think is the perfect boy/girlfriend.

4. Your parents give you the credit card and tell you to have fun.

5. You make straight A's on your report card.

6. A Hollywood studio is making a movie in your hometown and the director asks you to be in it.

7. You are asked to be a backup singer in your favorite music group.

8. You find a diamond ring in the bottom of an empty dumpster.

9. You discover that you can read people's minds.

10. You learn how to fly without an airplane.

ANALYSIS AND EVALUATION

JEWELS AND RAVENS

Rank the following from most important (or that best describe) the characters to least important for each character. Do this twice for each character, once for how they behave at the beginning of the story and then again for how they are at the end. Put a 1 for the most important, a 2 for the second most important, etc. (1-15). It is not necessary that all numbers change in the Before and After columns.

The Husband		*The Wife*		*Dove/Young Woman*	
Before	After	Before	After	Before	After
_____ Kindness _____		_____ Kindness _____		_____ Kindness _____	
_____ Creativity _____		_____ Creativity _____		_____ Creativity _____	
_____ Health _____		_____ Health _____		_____ Health _____	
_____ Justice _____		_____ Justice _____		_____ Justice _____	
_____ Love _____		_____ Love _____		_____ Love _____	
_____ Loyalty _____		_____ Loyalty _____		_____ Loyalty _____	
_____ Wisdom _____		_____ Wisdom _____		_____ Wisdom _____	
_____ Trust _____		_____ Trust _____		_____ Trust _____	
_____ Greed _____		_____ Greed _____		_____ Greed _____	
_____ Anger _____		_____ Anger _____		_____ Anger _____	
_____ Jealousy _____		_____ Jealousy _____		_____ Jealousy _____	
_____ Wealth _____		_____ Wealth _____		_____ Wealth _____	
_____ Sorrow _____		_____ Sorrow _____		_____ Sorrow _____	
_____ Fear _____		_____ Fear _____		_____ Fear _____	

Explain what each character values most in the story and why.

Explain how and why some characteristics change for each person in the story.

Are there any characteristics that do not change? What are they? Why don't they change? Which character changes the most? Why?

Of all the characteristics in the list, which one do you value most? Least? Why?

PATTERN WRITING

JEWELS AND RAVENS

An important aspect of this story is the fact that the husband and wife have reached old age and have become opposite kinds of people. What kind of person will you be when you get to be 80?

Make a list of the things you enjoy doing now.

Examples:

eating hot dogs at baseball games

spitting watermelon seeds

swimming in cool streams during the hottest days of summer

listening to rock'n' roll

playing video games

staying home from school when you're just a "little sick"

talking on the phone for hours

Make another list of things that you would like to be doing when you are 80. Be specific and go for the unexpected.

Examples:

wearing brightly colored feathers in your hair

riding in hot air balloons and dropping candy to children

wearing purple Bermuda shorts, orange tennis shoes and a lime green shirt

going to the movies and snoring

riding in shopping carts in supermarkets

having 37 cats (or dogs, or parrots, etc.)

learning to yodel

Use the items from your lists in a poem. Follow the model on the next activity sheet. Be sure that every line of the poem has specific ideas.

POETRY PATTERN

You know, when I get to be_____

I'll _____

And_____

And_____ .

I'll _____

And_____

And_____

And_____ .

I'll _____

And_____

And_____ .

I'd be able to_____

And_____

Or   _____

And_____ .

Instead, though I have to _____

And_____

And_____ .

Maybe I'll _____

So that my friends aren't too startled

When I _____ .

SAMPLE POEM:

You know, when I get to be eighty,
I'll play the banjo on crowded street corners,
And carry a pet parrot on my shoulder,
And whistle though my false teeth in crowded elevators.

I'll wear plaid pants
And great striped suspenders, flapping them as I walk,
And orange sneakers,
And bright purple shirts.

I'll ride in hot air balloons
And drop M&M candies to children and adults,
And learn to yodel.

I'd be able to steal trees from parks
And plant them in the forest where they belong,
Or go into movie theatres, fall asleep
And disturb everyone with my snoring.

Instead, though, I have to stay in school,
And hand in homework
and take tests and tests and tests.

Maybe I'll learn to yodel,
So my friends aren't too startled
When tomorrow I buy a banjo.

THE GARLIC JAR WOMAN
FOLKTALE FROM ROMANIA

Tasha's hands always smelled of garlic. Every day she left her small hut on the bank of the Prut River and went to the nearby forest. There she gathered garlic, brought it home and packed into clay pots which she sold to the local merchants in the town downriver. Tasha had been gathering garlic for longer than she could remember, and her hands reeked of the stuff. No soap, no matter how strong, could wash away the pungent odor. In fact, the other people who lived along the river no longer called her Tasha, but instead simply referred to her as the Garlic Jar Woman.

Tasha dreamed of better things and secretly thought that she was destined for a better kind of life. Each night before she went to sleep, she sketched a rough picture of a fine cottage where she could live free from work and worry. She cursed her fate of digging daily for garlic, cursed the ramshackle hut she lived in, and cursed the fact that her dreams never came true.

Unhappiness lined Tasha's face like deep erosions in a baked clay river bank. Her eyes, once a brilliant blue, were now colored with disappointment like a faded, hazy sky. Tasha's lips formed a tight line, never smiling, always on the verge of cracking. Even her hair, which had once been richly red, now hung from her head like brittle tree branches painted gray.

One Friday morning as Tasha was filling her bucket with clay from the river bank, she saw a strange image shimmering in the river. At first she thought that the sun was playing tricks on the water's surface, but as she looked more closely she was startled to discover that it was not the sun but was actually the mirage-like face of the River Spirit.

Tasha dropped her bucket and cried out. Then she hastily exclaimed, "I know who you are! You are the River Spirit! The legend says that anyone who catches a glimpse of you may have her heart's desire granted three times!"

The River Spirit spoke in a voice that sounded like water rippling over pebbles, "The legend is true. What do you desire?"

"I wish to live in a lovely little cottage that lets in only cool summer breezes and keeps out the icy fingers of winter. It should be a place with a fine thatched roof where roses bloom all year long. Do not disappoint me!"

The Spirit said, "Sleep tonight and tomorrow you shall realize your wish."

The next morning, Tasha awoke in the cottage of her dreams. As she opened the window to let in the cool summer breeze, the rich aroma of roses wafted into the cottage washing her with such an exquisite fragrance that the tight line on her face broke into a broad smile.

Tasha was content for a time. Very soon, though, the tight line of disappointment again creased her face. She called to the River Spirit a second time, "This cottage is too small. Besides it is too close to the river where the insects bother me. I should like to live in a mansion away from this river, where five servants will wait on me. In addition, the mansion should have beautiful windows in every room of its three stories, a thick oak front door with a bell on it, and a garden full of roses that bloom all year long!"

The Spirit said, "Sleep tonight and tomorrow you shall realize your dream."

The next morning, Tasha awoke in the mansion of her dreams. She danced through the rooms in each story, gave her servants endless orders, and lounged in the garden where she drank in the odor of roses.

Tasha was content for a time. But like before, the tight line of disappointment pressed itself upon her lips. She called to the River Spirit a third time, "This mansion does not have enough rooms and the garden is far too small. I think I should like instead to live in a castle where I have a hundred servants, where all the rooms are lined with rich tapestries and where I have a coach of my own so that I can visit the queen whenever I choose. Also, I will require a garden so large that it will take a day to walk through it. And it must have roses that boom all year long. Now be quick about it, and do not disappoint me or you will feel the wrath of my anger!"

The Spirit replied after a moment's hesitation, "Very well, sleep tonight and tomorrow you shall realize your dream."

The next morning Tasha awoke in the castle she had commanded the Spirit to create for her. Tasha spent many days ordering her one hundred servants to do impossible tasks for her. She visited the queen many times. She walked in the garden each night where the smell of roses hung like a beautiful cloud. As before, though, the ugly line of disappointment marked her face.

She called to the River Spirit a fourth time, "This castle will not do. I shall require that you create for me a palace so that I might become queen of the land."

The Spirit replied, "I have granted you three wishes. I may not grant you a fourth."

Tasha's eyes hardened into dull blue stones and her face flashed scarlet as she spoke, "You either grant me this last wish of mine, or I will tell everyone where you live and how to find you. Then you will have to grant so many wishes that you will never know a moment's rest! Now do as I command! And do not disappoint me!"

The Spirit answered in a sad, hollow voice, "Very well. Sleep tonight and tomorrow your dream shall be realized."

That night Tasha slept and was plagued by terrible dreams in which cottages, mansions and castles were crumbling.

The next morning, Tasha awoke. She was too amazed to speak, too amazed to be disappointed. Instead of finding herself as a queen living in a palace, she found herself shrunken in size and stuffed into a garlic jar which was sitting among other garlic jars on a merchant's cart heading to the queen's palace to be sold.

Whole-Language Activities for "The Garlic Jar Woman"

Before Reading Activities

Fluency and flexibility (p. 57)

The generative work in this activity sheet will give students a better understanding of the central and recurring motif in this story: Tasha's desire to live in continually better houses.

The questions on the activity sheet are designed to be cumulative in nature so that one question logically leads to the next.

Note: The activity sheet is also designed to help students become more capable creative thinkers.

Evaluation and analysis (p. 58)

1. "The Garlic Jar Woman" is another story in the long line of stories that revolves around the motif of a person being granted three wishes. This activity gives students the opportunity to put themselves in Tasha's place by asking them to tell what they would do if they were granted three wishes—the only catch is that students must include "roses" in their first two wishes.

2. Students are then asked to look at being granted their wishes in both a positive and negative light.

   Note: Some students may have difficulty seeing the negative side of being granted a wish; class discussion and brainstorming of negative possibilities will be an effective technique for dealing with this.

3. The final part of the activity is predictive in nature, as it asks students to look at what Tasha might wish for in a positive and negative way.

During Reading Activities

Comparative analysis

1. After the students have read to the point where Tasha is granted three wishes, they may want to stop and briefly think of other stories in which a character is granted three wishes.

2. List the titles on the board then encourage story comparisons by asking them the following questions:

   What did the main character in each story do to earn or be granted the wishes?

   What does each character wish for?

   How does each story end?

   What does each story have in common with the others?

3. Now ask students to predict what may happen in "The Garlic Jar Woman"—pay particular attention to the title.

After Reading Activities

Design studio (p. 59)

1. Design Studio allows and encourages students to think not only in words, but in shape, size and dimension as well. Students, like Tasha, are given the chance to create their own "dream house."

   Note: Because some students may not know exactly what to do when designing their own floor plan, one is supplied on the activity sheet.

2. In groups, students are to name each room of the house and fill each room with furniture. Using the floor plan as a model, students are to design their own house—any size, any number of floors,

any shape. They must label each room and also furnish each room.

3. The students might then compare their house with any one of Tasha's to discover similarities and differences—this will encourage rereading and comparative analysis.

Process writing (p. 60)

1. Using "The Garlic Jar Woman" as a model, students are to write their own story which focuses on a unique character, introduces that character to magical forces and details the outcome of the character's choices.

2. This activity sheet leads students through four stages in writing and encourages creativity, logical analysis and an organizational structure.

FLUENCY & FLEXIBILITY

1. Think of at least 25 different kinds of places in which people live.
   Examples: house, hut, cottage, etc.

2. Break your list of living places into at least three different categories.

3. Choose five places from your list in which you would like to live
   and rank them in order of your preference. Do the same with five places
   in which you would not like to live, with the worst ranked first. Explain
   why you made the choices you did.

4. Give five reasons why someone would live in a hut and write a descriptive
   paragraph of that person.

5. Give five reasons why someone would live in a palace and write a
   descriptive paragraph of that person.

6. How many things does someone who lives in a hut have in common with someone who
   lives in a palace?

EVALUATION & ANALYSIS

1. Imagine you have just been granted three wishes. What would you wish for? (You may not ask for more wishes.) There is one catch: Your first and second wishes must contain the word "roses."

    First wish:

    Second wish:

    Third wish:

2. One wish that many people long for is unlimited wealth and power. Make a list of all the positive and negative aspects of suddenly acquiring vast wealth and power.

Positive	Negative
(1)	(1)
(2)	(2)
(3)	(3)
(4)	(4)
(5)	(5)

3. Choose one of your wishes and make a list of all the positive and negative aspects of it (if it came true), then decide if you still want that wish.

Positive	Negative
(1)	(1)
(2)	(2)
(3)	(3)
(4)	(4)
(5)	(5)

4. What do you imagine a woman known as the Garlic Jar Woman would wish for if she had three wishes? (*You might first decide who you think she is, what she is like, where she lives, and what she wants/needs.*) Explain your answers.

    First wish:

    Second wish:

    Third wish:

DESIGN STUDIO

In "The Garlic Jar Woman," Tasha was granted her wishes and lived in a cottage, a mansion and a castle. If you were granted a wish and could create and design your own dream house, what would you design? Well, here's your opportunity. Draw the floor plans for your own ideal home. Be sure to do the following: label all rooms; fill each room with furniture that is labeled; mark all doors, windows, closets and stairways; and be as divergent and creative as you want.

Sample floor plan: Decide what each room below should be, then design your own house.

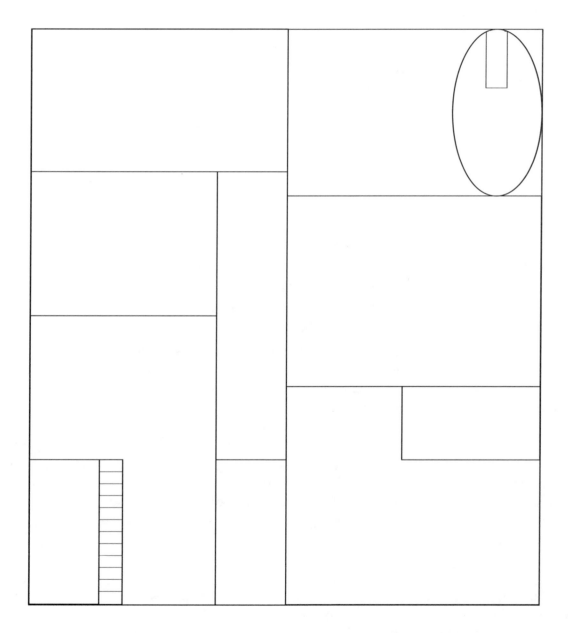

PROCESS WRITING

Step One: Getting started

Think of characters who might be modeled on the Garlic Jar Woman. For example: The Cave Man, The Bird Nest Boy, The River Raft Woman, The Book Shelf Girl, The Hub Cap Man, The Tunnel People, The Pumpkin Shell Girl, The Salt Shaker Boy, The Steel Thimble Woman, etc.

Decide what kind of person your character is. Consider: your character's age; physical details; where your character lives; your character's hopes, fears, desires, dreams, problems, joys; what your character does for a living; and your character's past.

Set up an encounter between your character and a magical force so that your character is granted three wishes. Try and have your character meet the magical force in an unexpected way. Also try and have the magical force be something that no one has ever thought of before. Then have your character ask for his/her three wishes—be specific and original with the wishes. What the character asks for should form the basic problem of your story. The way the problem is resolved is up to you, but try and think of a new and creative resolution.

Step Two: Writing

Follow the format of "The Garlic Jar Woman" for your method of development and organization.

In the first part of your story, set the scene and introduce the character. Go on to describe your character both physically and emotionally.

Introduce the complication—that is, the character's encounter with a magical force.

The character should then have his/her three wishes granted. This should add further complications to the story so that a larger problem develops with either the character or with the character's relationship with the magical force.

Finally, the problem should rise to a climax with the character's last wish. In many folktales, the character must use his/her last wish to undo the first two. You may also grant the character a fourth wish—but usually this fourth wish does not turn out to be what the character expects.

Step Three: Editing

Check your story for: A clear sense of organization—Does your plot develop in a logical way? Character development—Does your character act in a fairly consistent manner? Descriptive details—Do you describe people, places, and events with clear and vivid language? Problem resolution—Do you surprise your reader with your story's end?

Step Four: Final draft

Read your story aloud to a member of the class. Do you find any places where you need to either ad or delete words? Can you replace some verbs and adjectives with new and more powerful words? Did you use any similes, metaphors, alliteration, onomatopoeia, or hyperbole?

SILVER TEARS

FOLKTALE FROM COSTA RICA

The king and the country both burned with a mysterious fever. The king lay agonizing with a fire raging inside him. His eyes, normally dark and kind, looked like hot coals. Sweat ran in rivers down his face, while low, pain-filled groans escaped almost continuously from between his clenched teeth.

The country suffered too. Rivers and lakes had dried up, leaving nothing but stone-hard beds. Crops withered and curled into empty husks. The only wind that blew was as dry and hard as sand.

No one knew what to do. The king's physicians sat like wilted flowers and scratched their heads with disbelief. The fever had laughed in their learned faces and kept on raging.

Outside, people performed great rituals and ceremonies to break the heat and bring rain. Like the physicians' remedies, the rituals and ceremonies failed. The sun endured and the heat devoured everything.

One night Manual, the king's son, was sitting with his ailing father. The night was so hot that even the crickets had stopped singing. Manual carefully dipped a cloth into cool water and gently pressed it to his father's burning forehead. Just as he removed the cloth, his father's eyes blinked open.

The king gasped and in a raspy voice said, "Do you hear it? Listen!"

** How many different things can you name that you think the king might hear?

At first Manual thought that the king was just delirious, but then he listened more carefully. In the distance he heard the faint echoes of music so exquisite that he felt mesmerized.

The king whispered desperately, "My son, find that heavenly music and bring it to me. It alone can break the fever that burns both me and our country!"

Manual left the castle and followed the music through the night thick with heat. He travelled for hours until the first light of dawn revealed to him a great crevasse where the music echoed louder than before.

Manual found a rope hanging from an ageless tree. Taking a firm hold, he lowered himself. After descending for an hour, Manual felt stone beneath his feet. He found himself standing at the mouth of a vast tunnel burrowing deep into the earth. Here, the music grew louder.

** Will Manual enter the tunnel?   What possible things might he encounter there?

Eyes wide, hands extended, Manual entered the tunnel, pushing himself deeper and deeper into darkness. With every step he took, fear circled through Manual's mind like a giant panther. His heart pounded like a hammer against stone, and his body trembled. Squeezing back tears of fright,

Manual pressed on until his feet grew numb from walking. When his body felt rock-heavy with fatigue, Manual saw a glimmer of light and hurried towards it.

> ** *What could be the source of the light? What might Manual also find when he reaches the light?*

Manual cautiously approached a small fire in a circle of stone. Next to the fire sat an old man in a blue robe, whose gray beard fell from his chin to the stone floor. Before Manual could speak, the man stood up and turned towards him. The man's eyes gleamed with a mysterious light.

The old man said, "Sit, rest and drink."

As Manual sat, the old man handed him a cup of water. Manual downed it in one gulp. Immediately Manual's eyes brightened and his entire body felt relaxed and strong.

Manual said, "Who are you, Señor?"

The old man replied, "All I can tell you is that I am three hundred years old and that I have been expecting you."

Manual asked, "Can you tell me how to find the heavenly music?"

> ** *What answer might the old man give Manual?*

"Follow this tunnel. You will find a white horse that will take you to the music. And one last thing: When you encounter danger look for help in the eyes of the princess," said the old man.

"What do you mean?" asked Manual, but the old man had vanished.

Further on in the tunnel, Manual discovered a white horse. He jumped onto the horse's back and galloped toward the source of music.

> ** *What could possibly be the source of the music? What will Manual discover?*

Just when he thought that the horse could gallop no longer, Manual came into a dimly lit, expansive room. Seated in the center was a beautiful woman whose eyes were as rich

and dark as black pearls. Her hair was more radiant than a raven's wing bathed in sunlight; and her voice, which was the source of the heavenly music, was angelic.

Manual was stunned. Then he said, "Quickly, Señorita, give me your hand." He reached down and pulled her onto the back of the white horse. As they turned to escape into the tunnel the horse reared, nearly throwing Manual and the princess to the ground.

> ** *What could have made the horse rear?*

Barring their escape was a giant as tall as 13 men. In his egg-shaped head, his one good eye flashed a bolt of black lightning. Smoke billowed from his mouth, pouring over his jagged teeth. Balled into fists, his hands looked like roughly chiseled granite boulders. The giant bellowed out a sound like an entire forest on fire, a sound so great that it shook the room. He then lunged for the horse and its riders.

The horse bolted forward. Manual and the princess felt a rush of air as they passed beneath the giant's lunging hands. The horse galloped through the giant's legs and darted into the tunnel. The giant bounded after them.

The escape was a race of terror for Manual. Unable to see in the darkness, Manual heard only the sounds of his own desperate breathing, the princess' muffled cries, the horse's clattering hoofs, and the bellowing giant's thundering footfalls. Manual felt the giant's hot breath on the back of his neck, felt him growing closer and closer.

After an eternity of flight, Manual saw the end of the tunnel. Just as the horse broke into light the giant threw himself to the floor and with a last desperate lunge, caught hold of the horse's tail. The horse was jerked to a stop. Manual turned as he, the princess and the horse were dragged back into the darkness of the tunnel. Manual looked into the princess' eyes and saw two shining silver tears.

** What will Manual do?

Recalling the old man's advice, Manual gently caught the tears on the tip of his finger. He jumped from the horse, careful not to drop the tears. With his hand outstretched, Manual ran towards the giant who was stretched on the ground, the horse's tail still in his hand.

Seeing Manual, the giant's eye widened with disbelief. He raised his boulder-like fist, ready to smash Manual into oblivion. Manual was close enough to see the tops of the giant's jagged teeth and flicked the two silver tears into the dark gaping mouth.

** What do you think will happen next?

The giant screamed as the tears found their mark and he was transformed into steam with a hiss louder than a forest fire suddenly doused with a river of water. The hiss lasted an explosive instant and then was gone, leaving no trace of the giant.

Manual stood amazed. He turned to the princess and said, "How is it possible that your tears destroyed the giant?"

** What will the princess say?

The princess answered, "The giant was the terrible fever that plagued your country. I am the princess of a distant kingdom. The giant kidnapped me and held me captive because of my singing. I could not escape and only my tears of sorrow could destroy him. But I had to wait for someone else to throw them into his mouth. I could not do so."

Manual said, "Will you come with me now? My father is ailing and you alone can save him."

The princess answered, "Of course."

As they journeyed back to the castle, Manual noticed that the sun had stopped burning the crops, the rivers ran with cool water, and the flowers blossomed in rainbow patterns across the hills.

They reached the castle and hurried into the king's royal chamber. There they found the king still caught in the grip of the fever.

Manual said, "Father, I have found the heavenly music."

The princess began singing, her voice was as soft as a cool night breeze.

Slowly the king's eyes opened. His lips parted. Even his hands stopped trembling. The royal physician touched the king's forehead and exclaimed, "The fever is broken! The fever has fled!"

The next day a royal wedding took place between Manual and the princess.

Every night a new sound in the countryside mingles with the song of the crickets. It is the princess singing her heavenly music, music that will bring her new country peace and prosperity for many, many years.

Whole-Language Activities for "Silver Tears"

Before Reading Activities

Making predictions (p. 66)

In order for students to become more critical readers, it is necessary that they learn how to read a passage closely—that is, learn to read not only what a passage says, but also what it means.

Note: Meaning is created when students read a passage closely, think about what they have read based on their own experiences, and draw conclusions and make inferences from the totality of the passage.

Students are to read only the first two paragraphs from "Silver Tears" and then answer, either in groups or individually, the questions on the activity sheet.

Note: The questions are designed to help students use cause and effect thinking, engage in problem solving, draw inferences and make predictions about the story as a whole.

Vocabulary development (p. 67)

This activity sheet will help stimulate interest in language by incorporating vocabulary words from the story into questions that apply to the students.

Note: Before the students can successfully answer the questions, they will need to know what the words in italics mean.

During Reading Activities

Read and predict

1. Questions have been placed throughout the text of the story which will encourage students to make predictions and inferences as they read.

2. An effective technique is to photocopy the story and cut it into sections. Give students only one section at a time; answer and discuss the question at the end of the section before reading on.

After Reading Activities

Character analysis (p. 68)

This activity sheet will help students come to an intuitive understanding of the characters through associative thinking. By pulling from the students' knowledge and experience with contemporary music, this activity will serve as a bridge between the world of the students and the world of the story.

1. Students should list as many different kinds of music as they can.

2. After evaluating the types of music, the students should think of a song that can serve as a "theme song" for each character with an explanation as to why the song they have chosen is appropriate.

Writing with hyperbole and personification (p. 69)

To stimulate the students to engage in new and more dynamic writing patterns, this activity sheet is designed to introduce hyperbole and personification.

1. Since the opening passage of the story contains hyperbole, the students can use that as a model for their own completion of the open-ended statements on the activity sheet.

2. Since personification is an important motif in the story, students should be familiar and comfortable in using that type of figurative language in their own writing.

Note: The activity sheet offers suggestions for students to use in their own attempts at Personification.

3. The last part of the activity sheet asks students to personify other objects found in the story.

MAKING PREDICTIONS

SILVER TEARS

Read the following passage and answer the questions below.

The king and the country both burned with a mysterious fever. The king lay agonizing with a fire raging inside him. His eyes, normally dark and kind, looked like hot coals. Sweat ran in rivers down his face, while low pain-filled groans escaped almost continuously from between his clenched teeth.

The country suffered too. Rivers and lakes had dried up, leaving nothing but stone-hard beds. Crops withered and curled into empty husks. The only wind that blew was as dry and hard as sand.

1. How many different possible causes can you think of for the "mysterious fever"?

2. What other things, besides those mentioned, would be affected by the fever?

   a. add some details which describe other symptoms the king might have experienced

   b. add some details which describe other ways in which the country might have suffered

3. How many different ways of combating the effects of the fever can you think of?

4. How many different ways of ridding both king and country of the fever can you think of?

5. Where do you think this episode takes place? Why?

6. Is this episode set in the past, present or future? Why?

7. Do you think this passage appears at the beginning, middle or end of a story? Why?

8. Based on the information in this passage, make two predictions as to what you think the story will be about.

9. What do you think the title, "Silver Tears," means? What value, if any, do you think silver might have in this story? What value, if any, do you think tears might have in this story?

10. Think of a time in your life when you had a fever. Describe how you felt both physically and mentally/emotionally in a brief paragraph. Be sure to give specific details that appeal to sight, sound, touch, taste and/ or smell.

VOCABULARY DEVELOPMENT

Guess the meaning of each word in *italics* and answer the following.

1. When can eating your favorite ice cream be an *agonizing* experience?

2. If someone offered you the chance to become *delirious*, would you accept? Why/why not?

3. Which is more *exquisite*: a full dumpster or a fine jewelry store? Explain.

4. Briefly describe the last time you were *mesmerized*.

5. Would the flowers you just bought for a special friend wilt if you left them in the *radiant* sunshine? Why/why not?

6. Is *fatigue* something you look forward to? Explain.

7. Would someone who is singing an *angelic* song bellow out the lyrics? Why/why not?

8. Is it generally possible to *lunge* a thread through the eye of a needle? Why/why not?

9. Use the words *raspy* and *burrow* in the same sentence.

CHARACTER ANALYSIS

SILVER TEARS

1. How many different kinds of music can you name?
   Example: rock'n' roll, reggae, etc.

2. Rank the types of music you listed in order of your personal preference.

3. Which kind of music do you think each of the following characters would prefer? Give a reason or two to explain the choice you made.

   Manual:

   The Princess:

   The King:

   The Old Man:

   The Giant:

4. Of all the music you know, choose one song that you think would fit each character as a theme song. Give the title of the song and after each name and also a brief explanation as to how the song fits the character.

   Manual:

   The Princess:

   The King:

   The Old Man:

   The White Horse:

   The Giant:

Example: The Giant's song might be *Bad, Bad Leroy Brown* by Jim Croce—In the song the character of Leroy Brown, who thinks he cannot be beaten in a fight, meets someone who destroys him. The same thing happened to the Giant in "Silver Tears" because he was destroyed by Manual and the princess' tears—something that he probably did not expect could destroy him.

WRITING WITH HYPERBOLE & PERSONIFICATION

Writing with hyperbole: Complete the following

It was so hot that_____
_____

My fever was so great that _____
_____

It was so cold that_____
_____

My cold was so bad that _____
_____

It was so foggy that _____
_____

The giant's dandruff was so bad that
_____

It was so windy that _____
_____

The giant's breath was so rotten
that _____

Example: It was so hot that

...the sun sweated drops of fire.

...the sky melted and fell in globs to the ground making gooey blue puddles of sky-syrup.

...that we only added cocoa to the milk that came directly from our cow to make hot chocolate.

— —

Writing with personification

In "Silver Tears," the giant was the personification of the fever that plagued both the king and his country. Personification is taking something that is not human and giving it human qualities, such as speech, feelings, and thought.

Personify one of the following by writing one paragraph which is a physical description of it in human terms, and also by writing one paragraph in which the personified object speaks about its feelings or thoughts, its likes or dislikes, its hopes and fears, etc.

a common cold	a sprained ankle	a headache
a toothache	indigestion	a bruised arm
a sore throat	ringing ears	a stubbed toe
a screaming funny bone	a broken heart	crushed pride

How would you personify the following from the story "Silver Tears"?

the sun	the horse	the crevasse	the tunnel
the rope	the darkness	Manual's fear	the two tears

What other kinds of things can you think of to personify?

THE MULE OR THE DIAMOND

YIDDISH FOLKTALE

A farmer and his wife lived on the edge of the desert where the ground was dry and full of rocks. The farmer often told his wife, "If I were in the business of growing stones, I would be a rich man. But as it is, I must fight the ground for every inch of space to make even a few crops grow. Oh, how much easier my life would be if I only had a mule for ploughing and carrying water."

The farmer and his wife were so poor that they could not afford a mule. Each year, though, the ground seemed to become drier and more full of rocks. And each year the farmer worked harder and rarely complained.

The farmer's wife could no longer bear to watch her husband break his back when he worked and hoed the unforgiving ground. She took her most prized possession, her wedding dress that her mother had given her and which the farmer's wife was saving to give to her own daughter on her wedding day, and sold it in a nearby town. She received just enough money to buy a mule.

The farmer was amazed one evening to see his wife walking towards him, leading a mule. He ran to his wife and simply asked, "How?"

She smiled sadly and said, "I sold my dress."

"You sold your dress?" he asked.

"Yes," she replied, "but never mind, it was gathering dust and growing yellow. Look what I bought with the money."

The farmer was delighted. He stroked the mule's neck but stopped when his fingers felt something odd.

The farmer's eyes grew as wide as two large stones. "Look," he said, "look at this! This is a diamond hanging around the mule's neck."

The farmer's wife shrieked, "What? Oh yes, it is a diamond. Imagine, a real diamond!"

"Whoever sold you this mule must not have known he had left a diamond hanging around this mule's neck," said the farmer.

"What shall we do?" asked the farmer's wife.

For a moment the farmer and his wife remained silent. They were both imagining how their lives would change now that they had a diamond.

The farmer's eyes brightened as he whispered to his wife, "We could, you know, take this diamond to town and sell it. With the money we could buy a new plough, 10 goats, 20 chickens and two mules."

The farmer's wife whispered excitedly, "We could also buy a new cast iron skillet and kettle, a loom, a washboard and tub, and maybe even some new curtains."

Sweat trickled down the farmer's forehead as his eyes flashed with diamond light. He stammered, "Oh, and we could buy a new barn!"

His wife's voice fluttered like an excited bird when she exclaimed, "I could buy a new dress—no, ten new dresses—no, a hundred new dresses!"

The farmer then screamed, "And I could buy a new farm and hire a hundred farm workers!"

"And we would never have to work again!" shouted the farmer and his wife in one voice.

Stunned silence passed over them as they looked at each other with wild eyes, excitement still frozen on their faces.

The farmer swallowed hard and turned away, his face flushed.

The farmer's wife cleared her throat and smoothed her hair.

Slowly they looked at each other. Sheepish grins spread over their faces. They nodded, for the both understood what the other was thinking.

The farmer spoke, "We must give it back."

The farmer's wife agreed, "Yes, we must give it back. I paid the price for a mule, not a diamond."

Whole-Language Activities for "The Mule or the Diamond"

Before Reading Activities

Decision making (p. 74)

So that they will have a greater appreciation of the difficult decision that the farmer and his wife must make in "The Mule or The Diamond," the students should be presented with a similar opportunity in choosing between two equally compelling alternatives.

1. Present the questions on the activity sheet one at a time to the students. After students have arrived at an answer, they should state the reason for their decision.

2. After the students have answered all the questions, they should decide, of the ten, which question was the most difficult and the least difficult to answer—again they should give reasons why.

3. Students should then answer the last question on the sheet about the farmer and his wife.

4. Now ask the students to make predictions, based on the questions in the activity sheet, as to the nature of the conflicts in "The Mule or The Diamond."

Associative thinking (p. 75)

In order for students to gain greater facility in making associations between facts and ideas, they need to practice associative thinking.

1. Using the activity sheet, students should pick one of the nine figures that they "like" the most. Ask them to explain their choices.

2. Students should then answer the rest of the questions on the sheet. This activity will encourage both divergent and critical thinking.

During Reading Activities

Story prediction

1. Have students stop reading when they come to the part of the story where the farmer and his wife are trying to decide what they will purchase after selling the diamond.

2. Ask students to offer more suggestions about what the farmer and his wife might be interested in purchasing. Also ask the students to guess what the farmer and his wife will do with the diamond.

   Note: Students should support their answers with information from the text.

After Reading Activities

Character analysis (p. 76)

This activity sheet connects with the Before Reading Activity of Associative Thinking.

Students are to use the same nine figures in order to work towards a greater understanding of character. As the students choose both figures and words that best explain the characters in the story, they should also be ready to offer evidence. from the text as direct support.

Choices (p. 77)

1. After doing the character analysis, students should be ready to begin an investigation into cause/effect thinking about the characters.

2. For each of the decisions on the activity sheet, students should think of at least three causes and three effects.

   Note: This will encourage them to see that decisions spring from a variety of motivating factors and can also have a variety of results.

3. Students might then do the same kind of work on decisions they have made, or will make, in their own lives.

DECISION MAKING

What would you do if:

You were walking home from school one day and found a wallet containing a five dollar bill and the name, address, and telephone number of the owner?

Your answer:

You were walking home from school one day and found a wallet containing twelve fifty dollar bills and the name, address, and telephone number of the owner?

Your answer:

You found a diamond ring still containing the price tag just outside the door of an expensive jewelry story?

Your answer:

You discover that the bank had incorrectly deposited five hundred dollars in your savings account?

Your answer:

A travel agent gives you two free first-class tickets to Hawaii because she got your name mixed up with someone who had just paid for the tickets?

Your answer:

You see a sack full of money ($35,000) fall out of an armored truck. The driver of the truck doesn't notice and drives away?

Your answer:

In "The Mule or The Diamond," a farmer and his wife must make a difficult decision about keeping a diamond. What could be so difficult about making this particular choice? What would you do? Why?

ASSOCIATIVE THINKING

1. Choose your favorite shape from below. Explain your choice.

2. Which shape or combination of shapes best expresses your personality? Why?

3. Which shape or combination of shapes best expresses being wealthy? Why?

4. Which shape or combination of shapes best expresses a dessert? Why?

5. Which shape or combination of shapes best expresses poverty? Why?

6. Which three shapes are the most alike? Why?

7. Which shapes are opposites? Why?

8. Redraw the shapes, arranging them from most "important" to least "important."

9. Redraw and arrange the shapes to express the idea of having to make a difficult decision between two alternative.

CHARACTER ANALYSIS

1. What type of personality does each of these figures represent?

2. Choose words that you think fit each figure:

able	confident	gentle	lucky	heroic	skillful
fierce	cranky	blunt	vindictive	inquisitive	open
frantic	agreeable	happy	fragile	unloved	depressed
selfish	sensitive	trustworthy	poised	graceful	mean

3. Which figure best represents the farmer? Why?

4. Which figures best represents the farmer's wife? Why?

5. Which combination of figures best represents the farmer and his wife together? Why?

6. Which word(s) best describes the farmer? Why?

7. Which word(s) best describes the farmer's wife? Why?

8. Which word(s) best describes the farmer and his wife together? Why?

9. Which figure best represents the entire story? Why?

10. Imagine the farmer had kept the diamond. Draw a series of original figures to illustrate what he would be like.

CHOICES

Life is full of choices—sometimes they are easy, sometimes they are hard. The farmer and his wife faced a number of hard choices in the story, "The Mule or The Diamond." As we all know when making choices, there are any number of causes and any number of effects.

How many different causes and effects can you think of for each of the following?

1. The farmer decides to farm on the edge of the desert.

   Causes:

   Effects:

2. The farmer's wife decides to sell her dress.

   Causes:

   Effects:

3. The wife brings home a mule without noticing the diamond around its neck.

   Causes:

   Effects:

4. The farmer and his wife become intoxicated with the thought of being rich.

   Causes:

   Effects:

5. The farmer and his wife decide to take the diamond back.

   Causes:

   Effects:

6. The farmer decides to keep the mule.

   Causes:

   Effects:

7. *Try your own!* Your decision:

   Causes:

   Effects:

STORY INTEGRATION WHOLE-LANGUAGE ACTIVITIES

Vocabulary extension / Character analysis (p. 80)

1. Begin this activity sheet with a fluency exercise by asking students to list all of the characters from the eight stories.

2. After the list is complete, ask students to break the list into two or three categories—this encourages flexible thinking.

3. Choose the 10 or 15 most important characters and have students use them to complete the activity sheet.

   Note: This activity will encourage vocabulary development and also inferential thinking.

Sentence patterns (p. 81)

This activity sheet will encourage students to use and assimilate new language patterns.

1. Students should write about each story using at least one of the patterns on the activity sheet.

2. This activity will also help students to see what they thought was most important in each story.

   Note: This is the beginning of a "reader response" interpretation.

Associative and inferential thinking (p. 82)

1. Many students are familiar with the "five senses" poem, so the twist on this activity should not be difficult for them.

2. Students should brainstorm abstract words, list them on the board and categorize them.

3. Next, students should choose five or six abstract words that they want to use as the basis for their "five senses" poem.

   Important: When the students write concrete details for each abstract word, they should use details from the eight stories they have read.

Good news / Bad news writing pattern (p. 83)

Students will be able to integrate the characters, plots, motifs and themes from the eight stories with this activity.

1. After choosing one character, the students write about him/her in a "good news, bad news" format.

2. The character the students have chosen begins a journey in which he/she meets many other characters from other stories—but the first encounter is "good," while the second is "bad," while the third is "good," etc.

Inferring theme (p. 84)

This activity will help students discover how the idea of theme works.

Students are to read the poems, quotations, and proverbs on the activity sheet and decide which of those best corresponds to each of the eight stories.

Note: There is no one correct answer to this activity, so students must give reasons for their choices.

Associative thinking (p. 85)

1. To help students gain dexterity with associative thinking, they should look at the objects on the activity sheet and choose the one (or a combination of them) that somehow best represents each story.

2. It is important that students give reasons for their choices because they are interpreting the story through the shapes.

3. Therefore, it is important that the students talk about their thinking so that they gain a more acute awareness of it.

VOCABULARY EXTENSION / CHARACTER ANALYSIS

List all the important characters from each story below and answer the following questions. Be sure to give an explanation using direct evidence from the story as support.

Which character was the most:

assured	vindictive
stouthearted	obstinate
zealous	callous
fierce	creepy
repulsive	despondent
enigmatic	frightened
cautious	honorable
eager	triumphant
durable	trivial
authoritative	crinkled
arrogant	immense
graceful	raspy

SENTENCE PATTERNS

Read the following patterns for making sentences. Use the patterns for writing about each of the eight stories: "The Hunger for Music," "The Story of Mick McCann," "The Mule or the Diamond," "The Garlic-Jar Woman," "Silver Tears," "Giants & Mosquitoes," "Golden Silence," and "Jewels and Ravens."

1. Write a 20-word sentence in which you use at least ten words that begin with the same letter.

   Example: Perhaps Emperor *Po preferred* to be *poignantly pugnacious* because he *placed* his *pathetically pleading* guests in the *palace's putrid* dungeon.

2. Write a sentence in which you use at least three participle phrases.

   Example: Holding her breath, clenching her fists, and *hoping against hope that she was in the middle of a bad dream,* Tasha realized her last home was inside of a garlic jar.

3. Write a sentence in which you use an appositive phrase:

   Example: Mick McCann, *a wondering vagabond,* thought he would be safe for the night in the old woman's barn.

4. Write a sentence in which you use two absolute phrases:

   Example: Eyes wide, mouth open, Manual stared with disbelief at the terrible giant.

5. Write a compound sentence:

   Example: The farmer's wife *sold* her dress for the mule and then *discovered* a diamond around its neck.

6. Choose one paragraph from any one story and rewrite that paragraph in one sentence.

   Example: The king and country both burned with a mysterious fever. The kind lay agonizing with a fire raging inside him. His eyes, normally dark and kind, looked like hot coals. Sweat ran in rivers from his face flushed with red. Groans escaped from between his clenched teeth.

   Burning with fever, sweating terribly and groaning, the king was like his country because both burned with a mysterious fever.

7. Write a sentence in which you tell what three characters had in common:

   Example: The farmer's cold-eyed wife, Tasha, and the giants all became victims of greed.

8. Write a sentence in which you use onomatopoeia:

   Example: As Mick McCann walked to the old womans' house, his shoes *crunched* on the gravel and then made the boards of the porch *squeak.*

9. Write a sentence in which you use two similes:

   Example: The giant's *breath,* in "Silver Tears," must have *smelled like boiling grease* and *his eyes* must have *looked like black suns burning in his skull.*

10. Write a sentence that shows cause and effect:

    Example: Because Tasha was never content and wished to become a queen living in a palace, the river Spirit had no choice but to seal Tasha in a garlic jar.

ASSOCIATIVE & INFERENTIAL THINKING

Think of as many abstract words as you can.

Example: love, hate, greed, fear, justice, freedom, sadness, anger, jealousy, betrayal, trust, etc.

Write a five-senses poem about ten of these words using examples from the stories you have just read.

Example: <u>Jealousy</u>

Jealousy *looks* like the frigid grey glare in the eyes of the wife in "Jewel and Ravens."

Jealousy *sounds* like the anguished groan of the giants after they devoured the stuffed man's body in "Giants & Mosquitoes."

Jealousy *feels* like the wind blowing like dry, hot sand against skin in "Silver Tears."

Jealousy *smells* like a blast of stale garlic which erupted from Tasha's last house in "The Garlic Jar Woman."

Jealousy *tastes* like a single, stale, dry piece of rice that Emperor Po places on the tongue of one of his starving guests who does not know what the sweetest mucic is in "The Hunger for Music."

Try your own here:

_____ <u>looks like</u> _____

_____

_____ <u>sounds like</u> _____

_____

_____ <u>feels like</u> _____

_____

_____ <u>smells like</u> _____

_____

_____ <u>tastes like</u> _____

_____

GOOD NEWS / BAD NEWS WRITING PATTERN

Choose one character from the list of characters you generated in the Vocabulary Extension Activity to use in the following writing pattern.

Set your character on a journey during which he/she meets all (or most) of the other characters from the stories you have read. As your character encounters the others, he/she must encounter the first in a positive way, the next in a negative way, the next in a positive way, and so on and so forth.

Try to tie thematic ideas and/or plot motifs into your writing pattern.

Example:

After Mick McCann fled from the town of Donborough, he encountered an old woman on the side of Prut River. Tired and hungry Mick asked her for help. Because she was poor, she had no food to offer him. The *good news* was, however, that she directed him to the Emperor Po's palace where she was sure that Mick would find much exotic food and a comfortable place to rest.

Mick meandered for days through the countryside until he came to the palace that Tasha had spoken of. After being admitted into the throne room, he asked Emperor Po for some food and a place to rest. The emperor first asked Mick if he knew what the sweetest music was. The *bad news* was that Mick didn't have an answer, and so landed in the dungeon.

While Mick languished in the dungeon, he noticed that he had a dungeon-mate. When Mick asked his companion if he knew how to get out of the dungeon, the man, a common thief who was jailed for stealing a jar of olive oil, reached into his pocket and pulled out a single olive pit. The *good news* was that the thief had devised a plan for deliverance.

Continue this one, or try one of your own.

For a challenge, can you make your last sequence in your pattern the same as the first one?

INFERRING THEME

Choose a poem, a quotation, and/or a proverb that you think best expresses a theme or an idea in each of the following stories: "The Hunger for Music," "The Story of Mick McCann," "The Mule or The Diamond," "The Garlic-Jar Woman," "Silver Tears," "Giants & Mosquitoes," "Golden Silence," and "Jewels and Ravens." Be sure to give a reason for your choices.

Whether the weather be fine,
Or whether the weather be not,
Whether the weather be cold,
Or whether the weather be hot,
We'll weather the weather
Whatever the weather,
Whether we like it or not!

There was an old woman, and
*   what do you think?*
She lived upon nothing but
*   victuals and drink;*
Victuals and drink were chief
*   of her diet—*
Yet this plaguey old woman
*   could never be quiet.*

The lion and the unicorn
Were fighting for the crown;
The lion beat the unicorn
All round the town.
Some gave them white bread,
gave them brown;
Some gave them plum cake,
And sent them out of town.

Sam, Sam the butcher man,
Washed his face in a frying pan,
Combed his hair in a wagon wheel,
And died of a toothache in his heel.

Doctor Foster went to Gouster
In a shower of rain;
He stepped in a puddle,
Right up to his middle,
and was never seen again.

Birds of a feather flock together
And so do pigs and swine.
Rats and mice will have their choice,
And so will I have mine.

Fly away, fly away, over the sea,
Sun-loving swallow, for summer is done.
Come again, come again, come back to me,
Bringing the summer and bring the sun.

———

Prosperity makes some friends and many enemies.

Nature, like man, sometimes weeps for gladness.

The same people who can deny other's everything are famous for refusing themselves nothing.

Life is a jigsaw puzzle with most of the pieces missing.

We know what we are, but we know not what we may be.

A man is a lion in his own cause.

There can be no rainbow without a cloud and a storm.

ASSOCIATIVE THINKING

Choose the shape, or combination of shapes, that best expresses each of the following stories: "The Hunger for Music," "The Story of Mick McCann," "The Mule or the Diamond," "The Garlic-Jar Woman," "Silver Tears," "Giants & Mosquitoes," "Golden Silence," and "Jewels and Ravens." Be sure to give reasons for your choices.

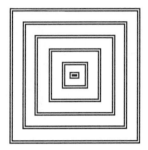
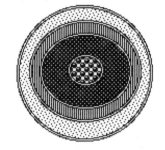
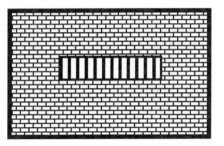

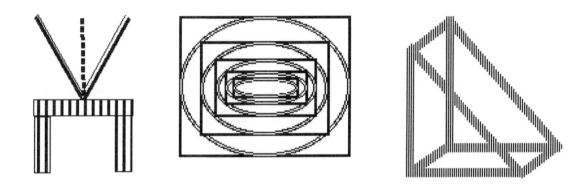

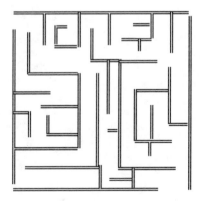
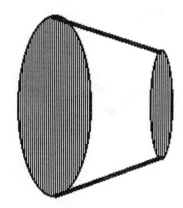

BIBLIOGRAPHY FOR MULTICULTURAL CHILDREN'S BOOK

Adoff, Arnold. *The Poetry of Black America.* Harper & Row, 1973.

Adoff, Arnold. *Malcolm X.* Crowell, 1970.

Armstrong, William. *Sounder.* Harper & Row, 1969.

Ashabranner, Brent. *Children of the Maya.* Dodd Mead, 1986.

Ashabranner, Brent. *Morning Star, Black Sun.* Dodd, Mead, 1984.

Ashabranner, Brent. *To Live in Two Worlds.* Dodd, Mead, 1984.

Beals, Carleton. *Stories Told by the Aztecs.* Abelard, 1970.

Bierhorst, John. *The Mythology of South America.* Morrow, 1988.

Bierhorst, John. *Black Rainbow: Legends of the Incas.* Farrar, Straus & Giroux, 1976.

Bierhorst, John. *The Hungry Woman.* Morrow, 1984.

Bierhorst, John. *The Whistling Skeleton.* Four Winds, 1982.

Brooks, Bruce. *Moves Make the Man.* Harper, 1984.

Carrison, Muriel. *Cambodian Folk Stories from the Gatiloke.* Tuttle, 1987.

Cisneros, Sandra. *The House on Mango Street.* Arte Publico, 1983.

Clark, Ann Nolan. *Year Walk.* Viking, 1975.

Collier, James and Christopher Collier. *Jump Ship to Freedom.* Delacorte, 1981.

Costabel, Eva Duetsch. *The Jews of New Amsterdam.* Macmillan, 1988.

Davis, Daniel. *Behind Barbed Wire.* Dutton, 1982.

Davis, Ossie. *Langston: A Play.* Delacorte, 1982.

DeFord, Deborah H. and Harry S. Stout. *An Enemy Among Them.* Houghton Mifflin, 1987.

DeMessieres, Nicole. *Reina the Galgo.* Dutton, 1981.

Dolphin, Laurie. *Oasis of Peace.* Scholastic, 1993.

Fitzhugh, Louise. *Nobody's Family Is Going to Change.* Dell, 1984.

Fox, Paula. *Slave Dancer.* Bradbury, 1973.

Freedman, Russell. *Indian Chiefs.* Holiday House, 1987.

George, Jean Craighead. *The Talking Earth.* Harper & Row, 1983.

George, Jean Craighead. *Water Sky.* Harper & Row, 1987.

Girion, Barbara. *Indian Summer.* Scholastic, 1990.

Greene, Bette. *Philip Hall Likes Me, I Reckon Maybe.* Dial, 1974.

Greenfield, Eloise. *Under the Sunday Tree.* Harper & Row, 1988.

Hall, Lynn. *Danza!* Scribners's Sons, 1981.

Hamilton, Virginia. *Anthony Burns.* Knopf, 1988.

Hamilton, Virginia. *The Bells of Christmas.* Harcourt Brace Jovanovich, 1989.

Hamilton, Virginia. *The House of Dies Drear.* Macmillan, 1968.

Hamilton, Virginia. *Junius Over Far.* Harper & Row, 1985.

Hamilton, Virginia. *The Magical Adventures of Pretty Pearl.* Harper & Row, 1983.

Hamilton, Virginia. *M.C. Higgins, the Great.* Macmillan, 1974.

Hamilton, Virginia. *The Mystery of Drear House.* Macmillan, 1968.

Hamilton, Virginia. *Paul Robeson.* Harper & Row, 1974.

Hamilton, Virginia. *The Planet of Junior Brown.* Macmillan, 1971.

Hamilton, Virginia. *Zeely.* Macmillan, 1967.

Hansen, Joyce. *Which Way Freedom.* Walker, 1986.

Harris, Christie. *Mouse Woman and the Vanished Princesses.* Atheneum, 1976.

Harris, Christie. *The Trouble with Adventurers.* Atheneum, 1982.

Haskins, James. *Black Theater in America.* Crowell, 1982.

Haskins, James. *The Life and Death of Martin Luther King, Jr.* Lothrop, Lee & Shepard, 1977.

Highwater, Jamake. *Anpao: An American Indian Odyssey.* Lipincott, 1977.

Highwater, Jamake. *The Ceremony of Innocence.* Harper & Row, 1985.

Highwater, Jamake. *I Wear the Morning Star.* Harper & Row, 1986.

Highwater, Jamake. *Legend Days.* Harper & Row, 1984.

Hirschfelder, Arlene. *Happily May I Walk.* Scribner's Sons, 1986.

Hobbs, Will. *Bearstone.* Atheneum, 1989.

Hudson, Jan. *Sweetgrass.* Tree Frog, 1984.

Hughes, Langston. *The Dream Keeper and Other Poems.* Knopf, 1986.

Hurmence, Belinda. *A Girl Called Boy.* Houghton Mifflin, 1982.

Konigsburg, Elaine. *About the B'nai Bagels.* Atheneum, 1971.

Krumgold, Joseph. *And Now Miguel.* Crowell, 1953.

Levine, Ellen. *If You Lived at the Time of Martin Luther King.* Scholastic, 1990.

Levinson, Riki. *Our Home is the Sea.* Dutton, 1988.

Levoy, M. *Alan and Naomi.* Harper & Row, 1977.

Lowery, Lois. *Number the Stars.* Houghton Mifflin, 1989.

Markun, Patricia. *Central America and Panama.* Watts, 1983.

Marrin, Albert. *Aztecs and Spaniards.* Atheneum, 1986.

Marrin, Albert. *War Clouds in the West.* Atheneum, 1984.

McKissack, Patricia. *A Long Hard Journey: The Story of the Pullman Porter.* Walker, 1989.

Meltzer, Milton. *Black Americans: A History in Their Own Words.* Crowell, 1984.

Meltzer, Milton. *Langston Hughes: A Biography.* Crowell, 1968.

Meyer, Carolyn. *The Mystery of the Ancient Maya.* Atheneum, 1985.

Millard, Anne. *The Incas.* Warwick, 1980.

Miller, Douglas. *Frederick Douglass and the Fight for Freedom.* Facts on File, 1988.

Mitchell, Barbara. *Shoes for Everyone: A Story About Jan Matzeliger.* Carolrhoda, 1986.

Mohr, Nicholasa. *El Bronx Remembered.* Harper & Row, 1975.

Mohr, Nicholasa. *Going Home.* Dial, 1986.

Mohr, Nicholasa. *Nilda.* Harper & Row, 1973.

Monroe, Jean Guard. *They Dance in the Sky.* Houghton Mifflin, 1987.

Morrison, Dorothy. *Chief Sarah.* Atheneum, 1980.

Myers, Walter Dean. *Scorpions.* Harper & Row, 1988.

O'Dell, Scott. The Amethyst Ring. Houghton Mifflin, 1983.

O'Dell, Scott. *Black Pearl.* Houghton Mifflin, 19

O'Dell, Scott. *The Captive.* Houghton Mifflin, 1979.

O'Dell, Scott. *Carlota.* Houghton Mifflin, 1981.

O'Dell, Scott. *The Feathered Serpent.* Houghton Mifflin, 1981.

O'Dell, Scott. *Island of the Blue Dolphins.* Houghton Mifflin, 1960.

O'Dell, Scott. *The King's Fifth.* Houghton Mifflin, 1966.

O'Dell, Scott. *Sing Down the Moon.* Houghton Mifflin, 1970.

Paulsen, Gary. *Dogsong.* Bradbury, 1988.

Poatgieter, Alice Hermina. *Indian Legacy.* Messner, 1981.

Posell, Elsa. *Homecoming.* Harcourt Brace Jovanovich, 1987.

Potok, Chaim. *The Chosen.* Ballantine, 1967.

Prago, Albert. *Strangers in Their Own Land.* Four Winds, 1973.

Schuman, Jo Miles. *Art From Many Hands.* Davis, 1981.

Soto, Gary. *Baseball in April and Other Stories.* Harcourt Brace Jovanovich, 1990.

Sperry, Armstrong. *Call It Courage.* Macmillan, 1940.

Taylor, Mildred D. *The Gold Cadillac.* Dial, 1987.

Taylor, Mildred. *Let the Circle Be Unbroken.* Dial, 1981.

Taylor, Mildred. *Roll of Thunder, Hear My Cry.* Dial, 1976.

Trevino, Elizabeth Borton. *I, Juan de Pareja.* Farrar, Straus & Giroux, 1965.

Tsuchiya, Yukio. *Faithful Elephants.* Houghton Mifflin, 1988.

Uchida, Yoshiki. *A Jar Full of Dreams.* Macmillan, 1985.

Whitaker, Muriel. *Stories from the Canadian North.* Hurtig, 1980.

Yates, Elizabeth. *Amos Fortune, Free Man.* Dutton, 1950.

Yep, Lawrence. *Child of the Owl.* Harper & Row, 1977.

Yep, Lawrence. *Dragonwings.* Harper & Row, 1975.

Yep, Lawrence. *Mountain Light.* Harper & Row, 1985.

Yep, Lawrence. *Sea Glass.* Harper & Row, 1979.

Yep, Lawrence. *Serpent's Children.* Harper & Row, 1984.